Livin
Gospel Stories Today

John Pritchard is Archdeacon of Canterbury and was previously Warden of Cranmer Hall, Durham. He has served in parishes in Birmingham and Taunton and has been Diocesan Youth Officer for Bath and Wells diocese. Previous books by the author include *The Intercessions Handbook* and *Beginning Again*. He is married with two daughters.

Living the
Gospel Stories Today

JOHN PRITCHARD

TRIANGLE

To David Day,
whose preaching always inspires

First published in Great Britain in 2001 by
Triangle
SPCK
Holy Trinity Church
Marylebone Road
London NW1 4DU

British Library Cataloguing-in-Publication Data

A catalogue record for this book is available from the British Library

ISBN 0–281–05365–0

Typeset by Pioneer Associates, Perthshire
Printed in Great Britain by
Mackays of Chatham plc, Chatham, Kent

Contents

Contents

Living in a sea of stories

The young homeless girl spent a lot of time in a West End square, trying to get into conversation with people and to make friends. It wasn't that she wanted money; she just wanted people to notice her, but they thought they were too busy or too important to take any notice of a little homeless girl.

One evening there was a movie première in the square. Crowds gathered; impossibly luxurious cars glided up to the foyer; cameras flashed in the crisp, cold air. Then the glamorous film star arrived with a wide, sparkling smile and a stunning dress occasionally glimpsed through the extravagant folds of her rich cloak. The cameras went wild. Everyone crowded close, but the little homeless girl grew steadily more indignant.

She worked her way through the crowds, ducked under the protective rope and stood defiantly by the glamorous film star. 'Look,' she said. 'This isn't fair. No-one ever notices me, when all I want is some conversation and people to recognize that I exist, but when you come into the square everyone crowds round and can't take their eyes off you!'

'You're right,' said the glamorous film star. 'That isn't fair. Why don't you come with me in future? I could carry you in the folds of my cloak.'

'I'd like that,' said the little homeless girl. 'What's your name?'

'I'm called The Story,' said the glamorous film star. 'What's your name?'

'I'm called The Truth,' said the little homeless girl.

And from that day on The Truth went around wrapped up in the folds of The Story.

Isn't that how it is? While the truth is often ignored, a story usually gets a hearing, so it's best for the truth when it goes around wrapped up in the form of a story. Then people listen. Stories are personal, immediate, involving. They feel warm, while truth by itself feels cold. They feel glamorous, while truth feels emaciated and unloved. But truth is vitally important or we sink in a mire of personal opinions, prejudices and hunches. From the earliest days, therefore, societies have passed on their truth wrapped up in the folds of stories.

So it's rather odd that the Christian world – which possesses the Greatest Story Ever Told and, within it, some of the best individual stories you can imagine – often seems to have lost confidence in the value and power of story. The classic form of Christian communication, the sermon, rarely risks the high seas of narrative, preferring the dry, overland route of doctrine and ideas. A Cambridge don once began a sermon in a service for college servants like this: 'The ontological argument for the existence of God has in recent years, largely under Teutonic influence, been relegated to a position of comparative inferiority in the armoury of Christian apologetics.' Hullo? Which planet was he on?

Clergy are often apologetic about their use of stories, seeming to regard them as really for children, or merely as illustrations of the main point, which is of course An Idea. But Jesus didn't really go in for Ideas; he went in for narratives. He wasn't so much a theologian as God telling stories.

I've become intrigued by the power and prevalence of story in our culture, and indeed in every culture through the centuries. Some years ago I began to study the way stories crop up in the life of the Christian community and how, when that happens, they invariably prove to be powerful vehicles of faith, whether it be in preaching, adult education, evangelism, worship, social action, young people's work, pastoral care, spirituality or the like. There's gold to be found by digging into this stratum of human experience. Put at its simplest – stories *work*.

But why do they work? Let's consider a few reasons. Firstly they work because we all live in a sea of stories. They're our natural environment; we live and breathe stories all day. When we get up and listen to the radio we hear news items told in the form of short narratives. When we open the daily paper it's the same – personal stories sell newspapers. When we get to work people tell us stories about what they did over the weekend or the latest crisis with the hamster. Work itself will often involve people telling stories of success and failure, of working relationships and office politics. We get home and the children are watching Neighbours, and later we may be watching EastEnders (or Coronation Street, or Casualty, or listening to The Archers). Over the meal table we'll probably share stories of the people, the incidents, the humour and the frustrations of the day. An evening meeting or a night out with friends will give us scope for another round of stories as we catch up with each other's lives. Last thing at night perhaps we watch a video or read a novel – narrative again. Even the TV adverts after the late-night news are short narratives or episodes, very skilfully put across in 30 seconds. We live with stories from dawn to dusk and beyond.

If this is the normal habitat for all of us, it's not surprising that stories give us a hugely exciting format for communicating the love of a God who put himself squarely in the midst of human life and experience. We have a down-to-earth God who can be spoken of in the most down-to-earth of ways – that is, in stories. Those stories may be of what God has done in biblical times or what he's doing in our lives – or the life of the world – at the present time. The story-form embraces all.

Another reason why stories work so well in presenting the Christian faith is that the Bible itself, the Christian source document, is essentially narrative in form. It gives us the Big Story in hundreds of smaller stories. The Big Story is of God's loving search for us; 'Adam, where are you?' could be the subtitle of the whole Bible. The smaller stories tell of the detail of God's dealings with his people, culminating in the key narratives of Jesus. The upshot is that 22 out of the 66 books of the Bible are in narrative form, and because those are the bigger ones, well over half of the biblical material is actually presented as story. And all of the Bible is telling the one story of a loving Creator seeking the love of his people.

It might not be stretching the imagination too far to conclude from all this that there's something basic about the category of story in the Christian faith, and that we might well try making stories central in our own communication of that faith. Stories are 'bridges' over which the love of Christ can travel to meet and embrace us.

There's a third reason why stories work so well in communicating our faith, and that is that they allow our own stories to encounter God's story in a particularly powerful way. When these stories interact with each other the result is that, in subtle or profound ways, we are changed. When our own life-story intersects with God's life-story in Jesus, it isn't possible to wander off and change a plug or peel potatoes. We're swept up into the passionate narrative of Jesus Christ and some part of us will be different because of the encounter. When, at university, my story collided with the story of Jesus I was shaken to the core and exhilarated beyond measure. I had encountered the person who was going to captivate me for ever; not a blond Jesus in a long white nightie with birds flying round his head, but that enigmatic young Galilean who seemed to have things sussed, who made God real and vast and intimate, and who attracted people like a magnet. He's the One who changed my life around.

So we don't listen to those stories of Jesus in order to be informed. We know the stories; we know what happens next. We listen to the stories not to be informed but to be transformed. When we put the stories of Jesus alongside ours and compare them, something has to give. Some part of us is up for renegotiation. The stories of God come to us life-size; they engage the whole of us, and slowly we are changed into his likeness.

In the following short chapters I have tried to take those stories of Jesus and bring them freshly to life. I've tried to bring them into closer contact with our contemporary culture, sometimes collapsing the two time frames into one. And I've tried to put our own stories alongside the stories of Jesus so that in some way, we may be changed. Whether or not you find this way of retelling the story helpful and challenging, I believe that *some* form of vivid engagement with God's story in Jesus is essential to the transformation of our Church and culture. This is a society that has forgotten its stories in the rush for a bright, shining, dot.com future. There's a drought of God in the land, and the way to find water is to listen to the Christian story again with hope and expectation, and to discover The Truth wrapped up in the folds of The Story.

Joseph – accepting the child

MATTHEW 1.18–25

Some people carve their name into the surface of history as with a gouging instrument on hot steel. Others, as with a light finger in a sand-dune. These last are the ones who have minor walk-on parts in world history; there for a moment and then gone. For example, Mary and Joseph. We all know them – central, pivotal figures in the Christmas story. But how much do we know about Joseph by himself? And how much do we care? There's a huge devotional industry around Mary, but Joseph, like the proverbial dog, had his day, and it was a very short one.

Yet Joseph is the unsung hero of this whole Christmas story. Without him the whole story could have faltered. Without him God would have had to move to plan B. And what would that have been?

Plan B. A little boy had once been cast as the innkeeper in the school nativity play, but he'd desperately wanted to be Joseph. He brooded about it for weeks. Came the day of the performance. Joseph and Mary came in and knocked at the door of the inn. The innkeeper opened the door a fraction.

'Can we come in?' said Joseph, 'My wife's pregnant.'

The innkeeper hadn't brooded for weeks for nothing. He flung open the door, beamed at Joseph and Mary and said, 'Of course you can come in; we've plenty of space; you can have the best room in the hotel.'

There was a pause. Then Joseph showed his true quality. He said to Mary, 'Hold on Mary, I'll have a look around first.' He peered past the innkeeper, shook his head and said firmly, 'I couldn't take my wife into a place like that. Come on, Mary, we'll sleep in the stable round the back.' The story was back on course!

God would surely have been ready with plan B, but plan A was that he'd chosen Joseph and Mary. And Joseph had just had the shock of his life. Mary, his Mary, Mary the calm, the beautiful, Mary with the impish smile and the come-hither eyes, Mary *the loyal, the true* – Mary had just told him she was pregnant! Unbelievable! The world shuddered on its axis – or would have done if Joseph believed it had an axis. Not Mary! They were betrothed, for heaven's sake, which meant at that time as good as married, but without actually living together and making love.

They met again later in the day and sat down over a coffee to discuss what to do. Joseph was still in a daze, but the more they talked, and the more Mary denied there was any other man involved, the more obvious it became what he had to do. He loved Mary dearly; she'd been his life since they exchanged that first kiss behind the camel sheds. But he had to divorce her. That's what happened to end a betrothal; it needed a divorce, and he had to do it quietly, in front of two witnesses, as the law allowed. So he left, leaving his coffee half drunk, not daring to look back at Mary, for fear he'd melt, either in anger or in desire.

And then came that extraordinary night vision! How do you say in everyday words that an angel came and had a word with you? Try that on your friends down at the Sheep and Goats! But that's what happened. In that restless night, tossing and turning as he thought through the events of the day, Joseph suddenly became completely alert and focused, with every nerve-end tingling. He became absolutely certain, as if he was being addressed directly by God. 'Joseph, don't be so proud. It's OK; you don't know just how OK it is! Take Mary as your wife. I'm the one behind all this. She's going to have a son, and I'll tell you his name: it's Jesus. Don't even think of an alternative. It's Jesus, meaning *God is the saviour*. Now go to sleep.'

And he did. The next morning he went around to Mary's and as soon as the curtains were drawn back he had his finger on the door-bell. 'Mary,' he said, 'You're not going to believe this . . .'

That's more or less what the text of Matthew says. Whatever you make of the Virgin Birth as a factual event, that's what the text in Matthew says took place. And there are two very important things to take out of it. First, that this birth is down to God. Whatever the human process he used, the deepest level of meaning in this conception and birth is that its originator was God. In the beginning, God created the heavens and the earth; and in the beginning God also created Jesus as a special life.

The other crucial fact is that it all hung for a moment on the attitude of Joseph. And bless him, he said yes, he would accept the situation and he would take Mary as his wife. So they went ahead and posted the wedding invitations. But it might have been different. The life and work of Jesus depended on all sorts of contingencies. What if Jesus had been in a traffic accident with a runaway camel? What if Mary had said no, she'd rather not be bothered with giving birth to the Messiah just now, if that was all right with God. What if Joseph had said Mary should have the pregnancy terminated, or at any rate he wasn't going to have anything more to do with them both? He might have disowned the child. That's the point. *And so might we*. That's the other point. We too might disown the child.

Christmas is that wonderful time when we enter into another world. Just temporarily we bask in a different glow, and old hopes are reinstated, and the world is a little less chilly. But if it's true that at Christmas we enter into a different world, it's also true that for Christmas to be authentic another world has to enter into us. 'Where meek souls will receive him still, the dear Christ *enters in*.' There's another world, one not made or bought by us, but a gift, given and received, fragile, mysterious, and utterly breath-taking. We only catch a glimpse of this other world; too much of it would blow our fuse, we couldn't take it. But this much we can receive. This much – *Jesus*.

And it was this much that Joseph accepted too. He accepted the child. And with that acceptance came a new world of possibilities. It certainly wasn't easy. The birth itself for instance was very basic, in the shed round the back of the hotel. Moreover they still weren't married; they were just (you might say) in a 'stable relationship'. And then they were off as refugees into Egypt (another vision in the night). Even after that, life wasn't easy as a carpenter in an occupied land, with a growing family. Presumably Joseph died young. He doesn't appear in the stories of Jesus' ministry. It certainly wasn't easy, but Joseph had done the vital thing; he'd accepted the child, right at the start, instead of disowning him.

And will we do the same? That's the Christmas question. Will we accept the child? Because if we do, we accept mystery into our lives and we realize that faith is the dimension which gives life meaning. If we accept the child, we accept the rest of his family, the Christian family, with all the flaws and eccentricities of its members. If we accept the child, we accept his justice, and the social and political implications of that commitment. If we accept the child, we accept his journey, a bumpy road to heaven which may take us through hard country.

So if we accept the child, we don't forsake the world, but embrace it with all the passion and intensity of the incarnation. When the Pope at the Second Vatican Council was presented with a document on sexual morality he took out a ruler and measured the page. 'Two inches of generalities,' he said, 'and four inches of condemnation. Is that the way to speak to the modern world?' No, it isn't; accept the child and you accept his love for the world and his commitment to it. We become a new creation, occupied territory, taken over by grace and gratitude, and committed to the world. *If we accept the child*.

What we learn from Joseph is the risk of acceptance. He could so easily have rejected Mary and the child for the shame they had brought on him. But he didn't disown them; he accepted the child, and the child grew and thrived in the home of Joseph the carpenter, until the time came for the child – then a young man – to take *his* risk of acceptance, which was of a much more dangerous destiny.

But for now, we stand with Joseph, who stands with the child. And in this child, born in the night, all of life is a glorious possibility.

For personal or group reflection

- What is, for you, the hardest part of the Christian faith to accept?
- Is there anyone you are in danger of not accepting because of their behaviour, values or beliefs? What might you do about it?

Further group activities

- Joseph disappears from the Gospels early on. What would you like to think happened to him in the remainder of his life? Use your 'baptized imagination'!
- Could Jesus have been involved in a traffic accident with a camel? What are the implications of your answer for what you believe about Jesus and how God works in the world?
- Share with the rest of the group how you came to 'accept the child' for yourself.

For prayer

- Enter the Christmas stable in your imagination and use your senses of sight, smell, hearing and touch to experience it. Stay there and watch as long as you can; don't censor what happens. End up focusing on the child himself. And listen.
- Pray for any families you know where there are strains and a lack of acceptance of each other.
- Meditate on the words, 'When we were still far off you met us in your Son and brought us home.'

Mary and Elizabeth – attuned to God's presence

LUKE 1.39–56

Mary was 14 and pregnant. What's more, she wasn't married. Not ideal, she thought, not ideal at all. Joseph had been a bit lumpish about the whole thing, talking about recalling the wedding invitations and cancelling the photographer. Fortunately, after a good night's sleep and something about a dream, he'd got it sorted in his mind. She hoped he'd be OK.

But it wasn't much fun being sick in the morning and having this weird craving for Earl Grey tea. She needed a break, she decided, a trip into the hills to see cousin Elizabeth, who was also pregnant. A chance to talk about nappy rash and projectile vomiting. Elizabeth knew a lot more than her about most things and was bound to have some old-fashioned wisdom. So off she went to visit her.

Elizabeth was hanging out the washing when Mary arrived. A woman's work and all that. But it was most odd. No sooner had Elizabeth heard Mary's youthful greeting, than that wretched baby inside her went for the high jump record. Elizabeth gave a sudden start, but then a huge smile spread over her face. 'Blessed are you, Mary; blessed are you amongst all of us; blessed is the fruit of your holy womb; blessed are you for believing that all this would happen.'

And Mary found her voice too, with Elizabeth. She felt safe, understood, supported. And the words came tumbling out: 'My soul is just bursting with the greatness of the Lord; and my whole being is thrilled with God my saviour. He's noticed even me, the lowest of them all, and I honestly believe that in future people will call me incredibly blessed . . .'

We call it the Magnificat. She called it sheer delight.

Two women responding from the bottom of their hearts to the greatness and the goodness of God. Two women whose whole beings (their souls) leaped for joy as they recognized the presence of God.

When did we last leap for joy, I wonder? I once rang someone up to offer them a job and I heard his wife shriek with delight in the background as her husband tried to keep a sensible conversation going with the archdeacon! When my football team scores a goal, my heart leaps within me – often because of the scarcity value of the event. When I listen to the five dropping notes in the slow movement of Mozart's clarinet concerto, my heart does a triple salko. When I stood under Annapurna in the Himalayas at 6 a.m. on Holy Saturday a few years ago, my heart leaped and laughed for joy in the stunning silent splendour of those 20,000-ft giants. When do our hearts leap for joy?

The baby leaped in Elizabeth's womb when she came within the magnetic field of God's presence, which was in Mary. And Mary's heart leaped with joy with the realization of what God had entrusted to her, and those famous words of praise tumbled from her lips. For a while the morning sickness had made her forget the wonder of it all.

What seems to make people leap for joy, in other words, is becoming aware of the presence of God. But we only become aware of the presence of God if we're attuned to it and ready for it, if the antennae are out, if the receptors are working. And the fear is that very often we've closed our receptors down, we're not expecting to bump into the living God. And so we don't.

Why is it that people's hearts leap for joy in football matches, rock concerts, mountains, concert halls and all sorts of other places, but not often in church, in prayer, in taking communion? Have we forgotten to expect God to be present? Here are the deepest things in the deepest places, yet God is strangely absent. Have we perhaps domesticated the divine tiger? Have we drained the tank of living water? Have we ceased to expect a tug on the other end of the rope when we pray?

Mary and Elizabeth were attuned to the presence of God. They lived in the force field of the Spirit. And so they were ready to be overwhelmed by the reality of God in that hidden life in Mary's womb. Mary had made space for God to act, and he did. Elizabeth had made space in her life for the forerunner of Jesus, and the child leaped within her when Jesus came near.

If we could make space for God to act, and become attuned to his presence, able to recognize the transparent moment when it comes, we too might experience the odd lumbering leap for joy. It seems to be the case that practice makes perfect. We need to practise the presence of God. To remember him in the midst of ordinary life, to glance in his direction while we're watching the news or driving to the shops or mowing the lawn. We need to do ordinary things in the name of Christ, and recognize Jesus for a moment in each other. Then God may break into our life and steal our heart away.

Sometimes that experience will be a moment of sharp pleasure, but sometimes it will be gradual, like a slow-motion leap for joy. The novelist Susan Howatch moved into the Close at Salisbury, opposite the cathedral, and she wrote this in a newspaper article:

> I was not at peace. I was too conscious of the fact that making money and being a success had left me unful-filled and unhappy. It was then, as my private world became increasingly dark, that the light began to seep from the cathedral. That extraordinary building which until then I had viewed merely as a beautiful landmark started to infiltrate my consciousness on a variety of unexpected levels.
>
> I gazed at the cathedral and the cathedral gazed back. It occurred to me then that I didn't know quite so much about the important things of life as I thought I did. Then I realised that I knew absolutely nothing about anything and that it was high time I stopped wasting my life and started trying to find answers to the questions I had always been too busy to ask: Who was I? What was I supposed to be doing with my life? What did it all mean, if anything? I gazed again at the cathedral and now I saw beyond the beautiful façade to this creation of supreme value, achieved by hundreds of people using their special gifts. And I thought if I was to postulate the existence of God, and if I was to theorise that he had created each individual to play a specific role in creation, then my task was to find out what role had been assigned to me, and then play that

role to the hilt in order to move into harmony with my creator, and thus into harmony with myself.

Our experience of God will often be like that – a gentle dawning of light, a touch of Christ, a recognition, a comfort, a conviction, a peace. But it will be enough. For one touch of Christ is greater than a thousand doubts and a hundred dull days. Our task is simply to be ready and waiting, to be alert for the presence of God, with our spiritual receptors turned on.

The child leaped for joy in his mother's womb. The child in us can leap for joy too as we come close to Christ, who was carried in the womb of Mary, for us, and for our salvation.

For personal or group reflection

- When has your heart leaped for joy? Was it in a religious setting or not? What do you deduce from that?
- Could you practise the presence of God more effectively?
- Look back at today (or yesterday). What were your deeper moods, underneath the actions and events? Joy, sorrow, frustration, satisfaction, boredom? Why were they like that? Where were those feelings coming from? Was God around? Did you fail to spot him? What might the Spirit be saying to you?

Further group activities

- If members of the group were to think of themselves in their relationship with God and their lives as Christians as a type of animal, what animal would it be – and why? For example: a giraffe – inquisitive and highly visible, but shy and nervous if approached; or a labrador puppy – full of bounce and fun, but vulnerable and not very mature. Share with one or two first and then with the group, and draw out the implications. By this means we get to some of the emotions we feel about our faith and our knowledge of God.

- If the group is able, share some of the more vivid experiences of God which people have had. Honour those experiences and affirm them. Ask what change they made to the people involved. Can such experiences be sought or do they just happen?

For prayer

- Pray to be more alert to the daily presence of God around you.
- Recall and relive a time when your heart leaped for joy at the presence of God. Enter the experience again and enjoy it. Then reflect on it prayerfully, and ask God what lessons you can learn from it now.
- Pray for anyone you know who never seems to experience the joy of the Lord.

The paradox of being a disciple

MATTHEW 10.1–8

Being a Christian today isn't easy. It's not just a pleasant, civilized part of being British, all strawberries and cream, sunlit lawns and ripples of polite laughter. It's a tougher business altogether because our culture is pretty hostile to Christian belief, not in active opposition but in passive resistance and a refusal to take it seriously.

A columnist in the *Independent on Sunday* wrote:

Organised religion has sunk pretty low these days, at least among people I know; the feeling is that it's just third-raters who get involved, oily little tin-pot careerists or neurotics, people afraid of the modern world. A twentieth-century Cardinal Wolsey would be a film producer, or a cigar-smoking advertising mogul. Sir Thomas More would be a regular guest on late-night talk shows. These guys were big-time; you can't imagine them organising coffee mornings or creeping from door to door irritating housewives, can you? This is my local church, these mild-looking people must be my neighbours, but I've never seen any of them before; religious people and pagans live in completely different worlds these days. The churchgoers

19

all look like the nicer characters in Australian soaps; calm faces, a permanent half-smile, slightly out of date, inexpensive clothes. The majority of women are wearing floral dresses to mid-calf. I would bet that there are no druggies or vegetarians in the house, or people who read philosophy, or tell really good jokes in bars. These churchgoers are people I never get to meet, people who all have the word DUTY branded on to their foreheads.

Would that have described the first Christians, I wonder? We have this image of the disciples being heroic, larger than life figures, huge in faith, and living in a continual wash of wonder at what Jesus did last time he popped out to the shops or went off for a night's fishing. But is that right? Were those disciples so unlike us?

Simon Peter: well, he started out OK, but he couldn't stand the heat so he got out of the kitchen. Big words and fine phrases but when the pressure was on he somehow couldn't even remember having met Jesus. Not so much Peter the rock as Peter the pebble. James and John: bumptious couple, these two. Red hot sometimes, but so arrogant at others. 'Can we sit at the top table in the kingdom?' Jobs for the boys. Sorry, lads – dream on!

Thomas: a literalist, always wanting proof. 'OK Jesus – just do that again would you, only slowly this time . . .' Matthew: built his reputation on the basis of 'anything you can do, I can cheat better'. You wouldn't buy a second-hand chariot from this man. Simon the Zealot: always getting hold of the wrong end of the stick. He expected Jesus to get out of bed one morning, buckle on his six-shooter and clean up the town, sending the Romans packing. He just didn't get it at all. And there was Judas of course. He really blew it. Talk about a bad appointment. Good on figures maybe, but way out on strategic planning.

What a shower! Would you trust that lot with the gospel? Well, Jesus did!

He summoned his twelve disciples and gave them authority over unclean spirits and to cure every disease and sickness. And these are the names of the twelve apostles: first Simon (who is called Peter) and his brother Andrew; James son of Zebedee and his brother John; Philip and Bartholomew; Thomas and Matthew the tax collector; James son of Alphaeus, and Thaddaeus; Simon the Zealot and Judas Iscariot, who betrayed him.

There's a story of Jesus returning to heaven and meeting Gabriel the archangel.

'How did it go?' asked Gabriel.

'All right,' said Jesus. 'I did what had to be done, and I've left Peter and James and John and the others to get on with it now.'

'You can't be serious!' said Gabriel. 'That crowd? They all let you down appallingly! How can you leave it to them?'

'Well,' said Jesus, 'I have no other plans.'

Those disciples were just like us, and we're the people he trusts to finish the job. We're the ones in the frame – well, nearly 2,000 million of us actually! That's a lot of Christians; 30 per cent of the population of the world. But how effective are we? We might ask: 'Shouldn't one third of a pound of salt be having more effect on a pound of meat?'

That's the dilemma many of us face. If this Christian faith is so wonderful, how come it's having so little effect, not only on the western world with its irresistible materialism, and not only on the Church with its depressing moralism and small-mindedness, but on us, with our multiple and repetitive failures? Jesus sent out his twelve disciples to declare that the Kingdom of God had broken in, and was pouring through the streets, and was even now at the door. By contrast it seems that we send out our church members to declare that the summer fête is on next week and the services are as normal for this time of year. I remember when I was vicar of a parish called Wilton, a young woman asked: 'When Jesus founded the Church, did he have Wilton in mind?' Ouch!

So how do we live with this paradox? This divine society, the Church, which seems so far from divine, so far from that vision of Jesus sending out the twelve that bright, living dawn. How do we understand all that? One answer is this. A pair of binoculars has, of course, two lenses. To see clearly we have to bring them into a single focus. As we look at the Church, one lens shows all too clearly the fallibility of the people of God, and if we forget, we have an often cynical and negative press to point it out to us. We're aware of the conservatism, the faithlessness and the sheer silliness of so much of what the Church does. We're aware of the tendency to concentrate on secondary issues, the temptation to institutionalize God, the danger of death by religion. We're aware that Peter, James and John have become Alan, Kevin and me, and we're all fallible and flawed.

All that is what we see through one lens of the binoculars. Through the other lens we see another picture. We see the purposes of God being irresistible, irreversible and certain. We see the resurrection as the stamp of God's victory over all that would distort and disfigure his world. We see the cosmic armistice and the defeat of evil, and the gates of hell shall not prevail. All this is absolutely guaranteed by our faith. No losing side; no depressing statistics; no mocking press.

So what we have to do is to bring together these two lenses – the fallibility and the certainty – into a single picture. And as we do this we find that it all resolves into a single image, the image of a cross. Here is a God who suffers as he heals, who dies as he overcomes, who shares the darkness as he ushers in the blazing light. In the foreground of the picture is this astonishing cross, and in the background is the hinterland of eternity. In eternity the paradoxes of our experience will be swept up into the wholeness of God, because of that cross, where Christ soaked up the evil and squeezed it out into the eternal mercy of God.

If that seems far-fetched, remember the tiny shoots of green grace growing up all over the back gardens of society. Those tiny shoots will eventually overrun all the concrete we pour over the spiritual dimension of our lives. I remember talking to a group of inner-city Christians about their spirituality, and one person said that the Holy Spirit was never defeated. 'It's wonderful,' he said, 'how a single blade of grass can bugger up six inches of concrete!' Grace is irresistible. God is irresistible. Love is irresistible. Because they're inexhaustible.

We probably find it as difficult today to take faith seriously, and to live it well, as disciples have always found it. It's always hard to make our present experience of frailty and bewilderment fit in with the great pictures of faith and holiness, a new heaven and a new earth. But there is at least a partial resolution to the paradox as we bring the two pictures together and find that they make the evocative shape of a cross. The cross is the beginning of wisdom and the still point of our turning world.

For personal or group reflection

- Which of Jesus' first followers do you most identify with, and why?
- If everyone in your church were doing and contributing what you are, how healthy would the church be?!
- Can you sense any direction in your discipleship, a developing movement of your spirit/God's Spirit?

Further group activities

- What's going on in the bad press the Church usually receives? What are the dynamics in the Church itself, in the media, and in society at large?
- On a flip chart, make up the front page of a local or national newspaper (in outline, not in every word) which reports the news of what God is doing (and suffering) in the world today. What stories would you put in, and what pictures? You could develop this with what features there would be inside; would there be cartoons? What would be on the sports page?

For prayer

- 'I've left Peter and the others to get on with it now.' Relish the knowledge that Christ loves and trusts you enough to share the task of redeeming the world.
- Pray for the integrity of the Church in proclaiming

God's good news. Pray that we may *live it* as we *offer it*.

- Pray for church leaders and their public presentation of the life and beliefs of the Church.

First principles

THE HEALING OF THE CRIPPLED WOMAN:
LUKE 13.10–17

One of my favourite stories is about a games afternoon at a secondary school. The rugby dropouts, those with two left feet and a hangover, are down on the bottom field out of everyone's view. They're doing nothing – chatting, lounging around, and being watched over by a prefect called Tompkins. Then the headmaster comes into view from the top field, and suddenly it's all action – line outs, scrums, mauls, it's all exciting stuff. The headmaster stands there watching all this for a while, and then he turns to the prefect and says: 'Tompkins, where's the ball?'

In other words, what's this game all about? Is there any purpose to it? It's the kind of question Jesus put to the leader of the synagogue one sabbath morning: 'Do you know what's it all for, this religion you're going on about? Or have you just missed the point?'

There are four individuals or groups of players in this scene. First there's Jesus – teaching, standing out at the front, authoritative, with good eye-contact, having that mesmeric effect he always seems to have. They listen, and all the grime and the encrustations fall away from the Jewish law and leave the purity of it gleaming and sparkling in the fresh, spring air. Then a woman, the second player, comes on stage, struggling in to the back of the synagogue where the crowd has gathered. It takes her such a long time to get here because she's all bent over; her body looks so brittle that you'd think she would snap if you touched her. Nobody does touch her. They ignore her. Eighteen years is a long time to remain sympathetic.

But Jesus spots her immediately. She's just trying to creep in to her place at the back with the other misfits (they're the third group of players in this scene), but Jesus is appalled at her plight, and right in the middle of his sermon, the words are just wrenched out of him, flying towards her, with healing in their wings. 'Dear woman,' he says, 'you're free of all that!'

Well, they're shocked! I mean, you would be, wouldn't you? Sabbath services are tidy affairs. You dress up, set the timer on the oven, and walk to the synagogue. Then you expect some nice tidy liturgy, some good singing (Shine, Yahweh, Shine if you're lucky), and a comforting sermon (short), preferably about the Jews being God's favourites.

But here's this Jesus making it like a revival meeting! Doing something distinctly untidy, and throwing their mental furniture all over the place. Healing this woman. Because that's what happened. No sooner had Jesus' words hit their target than she was unbending that crippled back, stretching herself like a ballet dancer, and then crying with delight.

So here comes the fourth player, the leader of the synagogue. Thank goodness for Benjamin, for a bit of sanity, a bit of gravitas. He's good at putting furniture straight, and he's clearly very upset at all this. But it's odd. He can't bring himself to talk directly to Jesus; he has to harangue the crowd at the back of the synagogue instead. Why is that? Is Jesus too powerful? Perhaps he can't look straight into the eyes of God. So he tells the poor unfortunates at the back to clear off. They've got six days to come and be healed; keep Sunday special – or rather, Saturday. The sabbath is too holy for mere healing.

Well I ask you! What was Jesus supposed to make of that? He really lays into old Benjamin and his cronies. 'You hypocrites,' he explodes. And that's just the start. 'You're quite happy to set your animals free on a sabbath when they need water, but you won't let an old lady, made in the image of God, a daughter of Abraham, have the same freedom that you give your animals! Get real! Get yourselves sorted out!'

And a cheer goes up from the one-and-sixpennies at the back. Yes! Give him another one Jesus! Not very edifying of course, but they recognize the shining reality of the Jewish law, not only in this man's words, but also in his power. This is what the law was always really meant to be about. This is real religion!

And I think I hear that challenge echoing through the centuries to us as well. Have we got it straight? What's it all for? Have we somehow lost the pristine clarity of this glorious Christian faith and smothered it with a highly elaborate religious game? Have we taken the gospel that gives a crippled woman a straight back and made it into an intricate system of rules and rituals, of dogmas and doctrines? Have we made a story into a system, and in the process locked out the sun? That's the awful thought. So what do we think it's all about?

We all have a Pharisee in us just waiting to pop out. We can all play a religious game with our faith, admiring the aesthetics of it but missing the blazing reality of it.

Enjoying the shape and sound of it, except when it comes in the shape of a bent back becoming straight and the sound of a woman crying with joy.

But if we miss the heart of it, the glorious gift of wholeness and life, the results can be serious. We're left with a shell of the faith Jesus meant us to have, a cardboard castle left in the rain. The philosopher Kierkegaard once described that kind of faith like this: 'a religion about as genuine as a cup of tea made from a bit of paper which once lay in a drawer beside another bit of paper which had once been used to wrap up a few dried leaves from which tea had already been made three times'. Some cup of tea! Some faith! Religion as a dull habit is not that for which Christ died.

And now the truth begins to dawn. Not only are we in danger of being the leader of the synagogue, protecting our little religious system as we like it and want it; we're also the woman with the crippled back. We ourselves are bent and distorted images of the God we want to love. We all need the touch of Christ, the healing word that burns into our soul and makes us straight. I am the crippled woman.

But Jesus keeps coming to us in every moment of the day, and offers us release and straightening. He offers us a straight set of values, a clear understanding of ourselves and of God, he offers us a straight path through the garden of good and evil. And he gives us the chance to join him in making the paths of others straight; to notice when others are bent and burdened when we meet them, to join in community groups and school associations, to get stuck into charities designed to straighten out the world's crooked places. I am the crippled woman, but Jesus can heal even me, and use me to heal others.

As we let Jesus make our bent backs straight, so we become an Easter people, with an ascended Lord, in a Pentecost church, sharing the glorious, liberating love of God. And *that's* what it's all about! It's about becoming people who positively hum with the grace and love of God.

For personal or group reflection

- What first attracted you to the Christian faith?
- On what occasions do you find yourself part of the 'religious game'?
- What is needed to make Christian faith more alive, for you personally and for your church?
- Can you share any memories of times where Jesus helped to 'straighten you out'?

Further group activity

- Work out, first individually and then as a group, what are the five key beliefs at the heart of your faith. Not just 'right' answers but 'real' answers. What 'works' for you in your faith?
- One or two of the group be 'devil's advocates' who don't understand what this Christian faith is all about. Can the rest of you (gently) help them to understand? (Don't worry if this seems difficult – just do your best!)

For prayer

- What is it in your life and faith that bends you over and cripples you? What can you never 'get off your back'? Pray for release. Let the love of God ease through you.

- Pray specifically for anyone you know who daily has to deal with disability or a burden.

Whose life is it anyway?

THE PARABLE OF THE RICH FOOL: LUKE 12.13–21

If you asked Jesus a question when he was in full flow, you ran a risk. He was quite likely to take your question, turn it around, throw in a parable, tie you up with it, and leave you feeling both embarrassed and strangely liberated. 'And who is my neighbour?' for instance. A perfectly ordinary question from a young man. He didn't know he was going to get the Good Samaritan for an answer. He was only asking for a simple tune and he got Beethoven's Ninth!

And that's just what happened in a story from Luke chapter 12. It's a simple request. 'Teacher, tell my brother to divide the family inheritance with me. Can you save me the lawyer's bills? He's being such a pain, and we want to build that little patio on the back of the house, and have a holiday down at the pyramids.'

But what does Jesus do? He holds this quite reasonable request up in the air, spins it round, and turns it back on the questioner! 'Take care!' he says. 'Be on your guard against all kinds of greed.' And then he tells a parable.

Always a parable. These little hand-grenades in the soul, that go off when they're least expected and change your life. This time it was about a farmer. He did well; made the right choices, got into barley just when those hot summers came and everybody wanted beer. But he was so successful he had to expand. He needed bigger barns and more parking space for the camels. 'This is it,' he thought. 'I've got it all sussed. I don't need all this religion, with those rabbis creeping around the village irritating housewives and organizing raffles. I can eat, drink and be profoundly merry. I can live as if there's no tomorrow.'

And guess what? There was no tomorrow! God met him with a full stop. 'And all those things that you've built up, whose will they be?' says God. 'Did you get it right?'

It's a parable with all sorts of subplots. One is about the transitoriness of life. Don't count on immortality, it says. There was a poignant picture in *The Times* of a young woman just finishing a half-marathon, and looking elated, fit, full of health. Thirty seconds after that picture was taken she collapsed and died, right in front of her mother and her fiancé. And they still don't know why. The post mortem showed nothing. Many of us could echo the sad discovery that life is a fragile and precious plant, so easily uprooted. But that's not what the parable is really about.

Another subplot is the seduction and deceit of wealth. It's true of course that Jesus was pretty straight about wealth, not because it's inherently evil – wealth is morally neutral – but because of its ability to seduce the soul. 'Sell all your goods and give to the poor,' he said once to an unfortunate young man who asked the wrong question. Why? Because in your case, in *your* case (and many others) your wealth is the greatest roadblock on your highway to faith. 'Don't set your heart on all these material things,' he said on another occasion, 'because where your treasure is there will your heart be also.' The heart is so easily kidnapped by good living and a good accountant. So don't fall for it, he says. And here's the same point in this story of the farmer who was rich in the world's goods and poverty-stricken in the things of God. But the parable isn't really about that either.

The parable is asking a deeper question still. And the question is this: Whose life is it anyway? Who does your life belong to? Has your soul been bought off by the glitz and glamour of larger barns, and a BMW and a good pension scheme? This parable is about where ultimately we place ourselves in the scheme of things. To whom are we answerable, if anyone? Where is our final security? Whose life is it anyway?

That's a very topical question. Our society asks it in a hundred different ways. When we tackle the vexed question of abortion, for instance, the question is there – whose life is this anyway? The mother's? The baby's? A divine gift? Or take euthanasia – whose life is this? The old person's? The family's? God's? The same question is there in the increasing fascination with the paranormal and horoscopes and new age spirituality. The question being asked is: whose life, whose world is this? Do *we* run it, or are there other forces? Even God perhaps? Many people want to know where their lives fit in. Who do we really belong to? Whose life is it anyway?

The answer given by the parable, implicit but loud with truth, is that our lives are on loan. My life is only safe with the One who truly owns it. It's certainly not safe with me. I wouldn't put me in charge of my life. I'd be arrested for dangerous driving. But our lives are on loan, and they're only secure when, as Paul says in Colossians, they're hidden with Christ in God. And then they're very safe. Once we can see that the 'eat, drink and be merry' strategy is a cruel deception, we might begin to recognize that our true centre of gravity is outside ourselves; we have a different home, another ownership, and we need to cease trusting ourselves, our skills and our good fortune, and instead trust the One who gives us our lives – on loan.

Once we've realized that our lives are on loan to us from God, we enter a world of freedoms. *Even if* our lives were taken tonight, we wouldn't be dismayed, because our treasure isn't stored up for ourselves and in ourselves, but is stored up in Christ. 'Your life is hidden with Christ in God.' We're safe. And therefore secure enough to be wealthy or to get by, to succeed or to fail, to change the world or to watch it go by. Because our life is on loan.

I was once taking the early morning communion service in Canterbury Cathedral, and there was an American in the small congregation. After the service he was clearly moved, and he said, 'I haven't been to a service for thirty years.'

'Welcome home,' I said simply, but meaning it.

'That's exactly it,' he said, and tears filled his eyes.

Jesus bids us come home, and to be 'rich towards God', not full of ourselves and our treasures. It's the privilege of the Christian to be rich enough not to need riches, to know the secret of a life on loan.

There's a story of a wandering holy man who settled down at dusk under a tree, near a big rock, beside a path, at the foot of a mountain. He was going to spend the night there, with a stone for a pillow. His meditations were disturbed by a businessman who came running up to him in a very agitated state. 'It must be you!' he said. 'I had a dream last night telling me to come to this tree, near the big rock, beside the path, at the foot of the mountain. Here a wandering holy man would give me a priceless stone and I'd be rich for ever. I've been searching all day, and I'm sure it must be you!'

'Well,' said the holy man, rummaging in his bag, 'perhaps this jewel is the stone from your dream. I saw it on the path the other day. Do take it.'

The businessman's mouth dropped open. The diamond was huge! He couldn't believe it. He carried it home, just bursting with delight. But the feeling didn't last, and by the end of the evening he was deeply troubled. He tossed and turned all night, and he couldn't get off to sleep. He wanted to plan a wonderful new future, but somehow he couldn't get that wandering holy man out of his mind.

Before dawn he got up, and he went back to the tree, near the big rock, beside the path, at the foot of the mountain. Disturbing the holy man's morning meditation, he laid the diamond before him on the ground. 'Please,' he said, 'can I have the precious gift that allowed you to give away this stone?'

This gift, the precious gift that enables us to live free of our obsession with wealth and possessions, is the knowledge that our lives are on loan. We belong in freedom to a Kingdom of grace and kindness, where people's value is intrinsic and underwritten by God. We neither despise wealth nor are deceived by it. Our hearts are simply fixed elsewhere. The anchor is secured in the love of God. When we know in our bones that this is our true home, we can eat, drink and be merry with the best of them, but we're not seduced by it. We could give away the stone, because there's something better behind it – knowing ourselves loved and valued, ransomed, healed, restored, forgiven, and secure with Christ in God. Whose life is it anyway?

For personal or group reflection

• Do you think of your life as 'on loan', or your own, or belonging to many, or what?
• What 'barn' is it that you are most tempted to rely on for security instead of God?
• What is the 'precious gift' for which you would give up everything?

Further group activities

• Someone says: 'All this talk of our lives being "on loan" is hopelessly airy-fairy. Unless you look after yourself no-one else is going to do it for you. God may be good for comfort and spiritual help but you have to live in the real world.' What would you say?
• Everyone in the group writes down ten things (tangible or otherwise) which they couldn't live without. Now go round the group with each person letting one thing go at a time; saying what it is, why they value it and why they are letting it go. When you are down to the last three things, each declares what those three priorities of their life are, and a discussion ensues.

For prayer

• Do a 'dry' communion. Hold up your hands and give to Jesus Christ your life, with all its load. Then into your empty hands receive your life back, on loan from God, and be thankful.

- Prayerfully and honestly, identify and confess to God your compulsions and false priorities.
- Give thanks for everything that makes your life worthwhile.

The table manners of the Kingdom

AT A WEDDING FEAST: LUKE 14.7–14

The trouble is – they had no table manners. Just came straight up to the top table and claimed it, like film stars. No questions asked, no permissions given. It was all just assumed, like some divine right of kings. 'No, Ruben, come up here! You don't want to sit down there with that lot – dossers and wasters, low-life and paparazzi. Come up here. There's more room, and we can catch the waiter's eye from up here.'

And Jesus watched them, and he said, 'Let me tell you about the table manners of the Kingdom.'

You've met them, haven't you? You're just sitting quietly in a restaurant with a friend, and in they come to the next table, with voices from the football terraces and humour from the school playground. They assume the world is waiting for them to speak, and when they do, they talk as if their opinions are an appendix to the Ten Commandments. And Jesus watches them too, in our day. And he says, 'Let me tell you about the table manners of the Kingdom.'

Many of us, instinctively, make for the top table, the best seats, centre-stage, where the spotlight picks us out and we sing (badly) 'I did it my way'. It doesn't have to be terribly obvious either. Most of us have our strategies for keeping ourselves at the centre. We can be tyrants by bullying or by whining. Self-centredness has a million garments, and we all have one that fits us perfectly. And Jesus says, 'Let me tell you about the table manners of the Kingdom.'

Many of us also have another strategy. It's the one that doesn't make for the top table, but goes instead to the bottom table. But we do it in a calculating way. Because there are different forms of humility. There's pious humility for a start. 'Did you notice I let Mrs Allsorts sit in my pew today?' 'I'm sorry if I'm a bit distant: fasting always has that effect on me.' 'I'm hopeless at prayer; I never seem to get more than one or two miracles a week.' That's pious humility – and it's false.

Then there's crafty humility. 'I tell him he plays better than me; then he buys me a drink.' 'I butter him up, you know; he's a complete idiot, but I might get that promotion.' 'Of course you know more about this than me, vicar, you're so good at these things. Now could I just mention that business of a church donation to my charity?' Crafty humility.

But then of course there's also true, Godly humility. The table manners of the Kingdom, that Jesus wants to tell us about. Don't race up to the high table, says Jesus. Go down to the lower tables. Start small. You'll find lots of friends down there, good, honest sinners, people who know their need of God. In fact, you'll find me down there with them as well.

Now this kind of humility is learned from Jesus. It's learned first hand from a man who never stood on his dignity. A man who was born in a borrowed stable, taught from a borrowed boat, fed 5,000 people with borrowed food, rode into Jerusalem on a borrowed donkey, celebrated the Last Supper in a borrowed room, borrowed the strength of a stranger to carry his cross, and was even buried in a borrowed tomb. You're not going to see Jesus pushing in to get the best seat.

What we're dealing with here is a God who washes feet. And that idea still scandalizes us, as it scandalized Peter at their last meal together. A God who washes feet. *A God who is humble*. Doesn't that take your breath away? A God who's powerful, beautiful, awesome, stunning – that's fine. A God who is colourful, creative, patient, full of mercy – no problem. But a God who is *humble*? Can we believe that?

A man once asked his rabbi: 'Why can't people see the face of God any more?'

The rabbi answered: 'It seems that no-one can stoop that low.'

Oh, that we, God's people, would take that lesson to heart! Because when the tide goes out, what should be left on the shore is humility and holiness. That's what the world wants of Christians. People don't want clever-dick answers, neat political foot-work, the Church's latest attempt to catch up with the nineteenth century. What they want is holiness. What they want is God, a glimpse of the beyond, a glimpse of something else. And they probably have to see it in us, or not at all. If they get the same loud-mouthed swaggering that they see in so many other parts of our culture, if they see in the church a backbiting community, arrogant and hypocritical, then they'll see not an icon of God, but a mirror-image of the larger culture of which we're all part. And they'll turn sadly away. Because what they want is humility and holiness – the table manners of the Kingdom.

We need to remember that the Kingdom of God starts

here and now. Jesus was talking at two levels, as so often. The Kingdom now, and the Kingdom then, in the future. You can't book your seats in the Kingdom of God in advance with a celestial credit card. The house rules are always the same. And one of the basic house rules in the Kingdom is this, says Jesus. 'Those who exalt themselves will be humbled, and those who humble themselves will be exalted.' What we have to learn from all this is that *exaltation comes by invitation only*. There's nothing we can do to buy our way into the club. So let Jesus tell us the table manners of the Kingdom. Let's learn them from him. And to help us, we can see them lived out in him, the God who washes feet.

Some years ago the Indian President Jawaharlal Nehru invited the film director David Lean and the wartime hero Leonard Cheshire to tea in Government House. At the time Cheshire was desperate to get hold of a piece of land in northern India to build one of his Cheshire Homes for the incurably sick, but foreigners were forbidden to own land and he was getting nowhere. During tea Cheshire was overcome by shyness and he didn't say a word, though he was aware he was in the presence of the one man who could really help him.

When it was time to leave, Nehru asked Cheshire how he was going to get back to his hotel, and he said he would take a bus or a tram and then walk. Nehru ordered his own car, saw Cheshire into it, and stood waving until it was out of sight – an unheard-of thing to do. Then he turned to an aide, and with tears in his eyes he said: 'That is the greatest man I have met since Gandhi. Give him the land that I know he wants.'

Exaltation comes by invitation only.

The table manners of the Kingdom don't fit very easily

with a world of image, style and glitz, spin-doctors and make-overs, a world where money maketh man, not manners. Following a downwardly mobile saviour on his way of the cross doesn't sound like a PR man's dream. But I know who'll be there at the end of the line, when the images are all broken, and the glitz has gone shoddy and the spin-doctor has spun out of sight. I know who I trust to have got it right, whose teaching is always spot on, and whose table manners are faultless.

This is what he said: 'Those who exalt themselves will be humbled, and those who humble themselves will be exalted.' Because exaltation comes by invitation only.

And the humble know it.

For personal or group reflection

- Where does your pride or pushiness still assert itself?
- Is it possible to *try* to become humble – or if you succeeded would that just make you proud another way?!
- Can a humble person avoid being walked over?

Further group activities

- Share some cameos or pen-pictures of people you have known who had that quality of humility.
- Brainstorm on a large sheet of paper the words which come to mind to describe the character of Jesus. Does 'humility' fit in with these words and ideas?
- How could your church start to practise feet-washing?

For prayer

- St Teresa of Avila taught that we should let Jesus look

at us 'lovingly and humbly'. Try that, with sincerity
and persistence.

- Meditate on the description of Jesus as a man who 'was
  born in a borrowed stable, taught from a borrowed
  boat, fed the 5,000 with borrowed food, rode into
  Jerusalem on a borrowed donkey, celebrated the Last
  Supper in a borrowed room, borrowed the strength
  of a stranger to carry his cross, and was buried in a
  borrowed tomb'.
- Pray for some of the quieter people you know, those
  who don't make a fuss but get on with their faith and
  life with a quiet dignity.

Playing the long game
(Why do bad people continue to flourish?)

THE WHEAT AND THE TARES: MATTHEW 13.24–30

There are some questions that we're not going to sort out until the last trump. Like – who really was William Shakespeare? Or – was the 1956 Manchester United line-up the best team ever? Or – why is there always a teaspoon left at the bottom of the washing-up bowl?

But some questions are rather more significant than those, and chief among them must be this: why do bad people continue to flourish? If God really is as concerned with issues of justice and fairness as his press releases make out, then why do bad people get away with it? Surely there must have been a case for a stray meteorite taking out Adolf Hitler. Or surely a divine arm-lock could have been put on Napoleon, or an off-duty angel could have deflected the bullets that killed John Kennedy.

'It's not fair,' we say, as one of our very first sentences in life, repeating and refining the sentiment throughout our lives. (And a young man on a cross says: 'Who said anything about fair?') But it is a puzzle. Why do bad people prosper?

Jesus once tackled the problem. He gave them a parable of course, another of those spiritual fireworks which he

45

threw into his disciples' lives, just to see if they were awake. There was this man (he said) with a few acres of land to plant, so he bought his packet of wheat seed and he read the European regulations on the size, colour, texture, weight, smell, ethnic origin, and star sign of those wheat seeds, and then he planted them.

But then his neighbour crept through the hedge at night and distributed ground elder and black bindweed and red deadnettle and other noxious weeds – and the whole wheat project went pear-shaped.

His farm manager was outraged. 'What shall we do?' he said. Torch the neighbour's farm? Tie him up in front of the Jerry Springer Show until madness ensues? Or simply go and collect all the weeds for a giant bonfire?

None of those things, says the landowner. Don't do anything yet. Let the wheat and the weeds grow together. We're playing the long game. We'll sort it all out when the time is right, when it's time for the Great Harvest Supper, the meal at the end of the world.

That's what Jesus said, or something like it. Because it was a problem in his time too. Why do evil people prosper? Come on Jesus; you've been promising that the Kingdom of God is just about to burst through the door, the great Shake Down, the Final Identity Parade, the Big Roll Call. But we don't see it! Herod is still around. Pilate is still preening himself at Caesarea. The Pharisees still have us tied up in religious knots. So what's going on? 'Why do bad people win the Lottery week by week?' they said. And they still say it.

Now there are a number of partial answers to this question in the parable itself. The first is this: you can't sort out the wheat from the weeds at this stage; they're indistinguishable. You can't just sort out the bad guys from the good guys. That's *Star Wars* and *Lord of the Rings*; it's not real life. Real life is more complex. And particularly in this; the line between the bad guys and the good guys runs right through each of us. We've not got it sussed. Or if you have, would you write and tell me how you do it? My life is a heap of ideals and compromises, of good intentions and embarrassing failures. I aim for the sky and eat the gravel.

There's a second partial answer to the question why bad people flourish. Jesus said, 'An enemy has done this.' Christians have long taken some comfort from blaming evil or the devil for being an active force working in opposition to the word and works of God. And certainly our experience of total evil in a civilized country (Nazi Germany), or appalling genocide in one of the most Christianized countries in Africa (Rwanda), or the way we're fascinated by evil deeds and tragedies in the press, or the way we identify with the primeval terror of horror movies – all this suggests the existence of a source of evil that men and women have often called the devil.

Now, they may well be right. And if you are happy with that explanation – fine. However, it may be that for some people that answer doesn't help. It may seem like an excuse. 'An enemy has done this,' people say. 'It's the devil up to his old tricks.' It couldn't possibly be our society choosing its own wealth rather than justice for the poor. It couldn't possibly be our culture exhibiting deep, inbuilt racism. It's nothing to do with me and my obstinacy or selfishness or downright choice to do wrong. The devil can therefore be a convenient receptacle for our own failures.

An alternative view might be that evil is the dreadful

absence of the loving presence of God. There is only one ultimate reality – God. We're not dualists, believing in God and the Devil forever slugging it out in the boxing ring of the world. We're monotheists – we believe in one God. So evil, on this view, is the inevitable consequence of anything which gets divorced from God. It's the potent absence of good rather than the active presence of the devil.

Whichever view we take, however, like Jesus, we must never underestimate the active power of evil. The point is not to debate the source of evil but to resist the reality of it. When I was going to bed at 14,000 feet at Annapurna Base Camp in the Himalayas a few years ago, and I was crawling semi-clothed into a freezing sleeping bag, it wouldn't have helped me much to tell me that cold wasn't a positive force but only the absence of the sun's warmth. The reality I experienced was like an invading flood of bitter cold, and that's what I had to deal with.

There's a third partial answer given in this parable to the conundrum of bad people prospering in a world made by a good God. And that answer is that God is playing the long game. The wheat is growing gradually. Let it grow. The Kingdom is steadily on its way. Nothing can stop it. Don't worry. It may seem slow, but that's often the speed of the Kingdom because that's the speed of love. A Japanese theologian wrote: 'God walks slowly because he is love. If he were not love he would have gone much faster. Love has its speed. It's an inner speed. It's a spiritual speed. It's a different speed from the technological speed to which we are accustomed. It goes on in the depths of our life, whether we notice or not, at three miles an hour. It's the speed we walk, and therefore it's the speed the love of God walks.'

God's victory, the victory of love (the wheat in our parable) is not in doubt, fragile and vulnerable as it may seem. God is patient; he works deeply. As John V. Taylor says: 'The truth about God is not so much that he is omnipotent as that he is inexhaustible. And for that reason, he will always succeed.'

I remember being high up in the Alps at the Rhône glacier and seeing the melt-water dripping from the end of the glacier so slowly it was almost painful. But then the water began its long journey down the mountain, gaining volume, gaining speed, gaining confidence, until eventually we could see it dancing, roaring and cascading through a gorge, gouging out a deep slice, like a knife through butter – except that it had taken millions of years to do. And finally the mighty river Rhône, deep, dark and majestic, flowed down the centre of France. And all from those faltering drops of water from the glacier high up in the mountains.

A parable? Yes, of the ceaseless, inexhaustible love of God, ever inventive and adaptable, possessing no other force except persistence. But God will achieve his goal in creation. He has all the patience in the world. The wheat of the Kingdom will grow steadily and patiently, and nothing will stop it. The love of God will wear away the damage to the human soul, never giving up until Christ is formed in us.

All of these partial answers help us to understand why bad people prosper, but the final answer Jesus gives to the persistence of evil is this: 'The end will come and it's in my hands. Trust me. The reapers will sort it out at the end. Don't anticipate the harvest; that's not in your hands. You just get on with what the Lord asks of you, here and now and happily. Just walk the walk while you're here. Love God and love your neighbour; follow Christ and be full of the Spirit.'

At the End it *will* be sorted, and it *will* be just, and it *will* be merciful, and it will be Christ who is all in all. All shall be well, and all manner of things shall be well.

To which we can only say – Alleluia! So be it!

For personal or group reflection

- Who do you think doesn't deserve to flourish – but does? Be honest! And why do you think that?
- If both wheat and weeds are growing in us all the time, what does the overall balance of them in your own life feel like at present? How healthy is the wheat? How do you keep the weeds down?
- 'God is not so much omnipotent as inexhaustible.' How do you feel about that statement?

Further group activities

- Divide into groups of four. In each group, one person takes the part of a psychiatrist, one an atheist, one a conservative Christian, one a more radical Christian. Discuss the evidence for the devil and his demons, starting with an opening statement from each person.
- In the chapter there are four partial answers to the problem of why bad people prosper. How satisfactory do you find those answers on a score of 1–10? Each person should write down their 'mark' separately, and then discuss together.

For prayer

- In your mind's eye, imagine your life laid out as a field full of wheat and weeds. Identify the wheat – the good, strong growth in your life – and give thanks for it. Identify the weeds – the failure, the 'undergrowth' – and ask for God's mercy.
- 'The ceaseless, inexhaustible love of God.' Bathe in that love silently for as long as you can.
- Pray that every person in your church may know that God loves them. Or pray for one or two people you know who particularly need that confidence.

Where do we stand in the story?

THE HEALING OF THE MAN BORN BLIND: JOHN 9

In the Gospels you sometimes become aware of a number of different angles on the same incident, each one significantly different in perception, depending on which person's eyes you're looking through. And the question we are then often faced with is this: what angle do we ourselves have on this particular story? Where do we position ourselves around Jesus?

Take a scene from John chapter 9. Here's Jesus, out for a walk on a Saturday afternoon, minding his own business, when he spots this man who's been blind since day one. Jesus and the blind man – centre stage. Meanwhile, stage left, the Pharisees, equipped with mobiles and lap-tops, ready to get the latest indiscretion from this dangerous Galilean out to the world's press. Stage right, the disciples, still blinking in the light of this extraordinary man they've got caught up with. And nearby, but in the shadows, the blind man's parents, ready for a small walk-on part, a cameo role about two people who don't want to get into trouble, and so keep on saying, 'Don't ask us, ask him! He's old enough; he can go into pubs.'

And off-stage, the crowd – millions of us, looking on

through the centuries, saints and scholars, students and artists, agnostics and wistful seekers. And us, reading the story now, where do we stand?

Let's start with the disciples. They want to ask theological questions, as do many of us. 'OK Jesus, let's take this blind man as a test case. Why is he blind? Was it his own sin or the sin of his parents?' Or as we might say, why did my friend die of cancer at 37? Why did those thousands get macheted to death in Rwanda? Why was that child born with brain damage? What did they do to deserve this?

And Jesus says, in effect: it's not their fault or God's fault. In a sense it's nobody's fault. It's the way the world is. It's the price we pay for a real world, with freedom and choice, without divine coercion. God gives his whole creation a radical freedom to be the way it is, without arbitrary intervention. But such a creation has the inevitable possibility of going wrong.

And yet in every case where something goes wrong we have the chance of seeing God at work, bringing good out of evil, throwing light into the darkness, turning the fast ball to the boundary. 'He was born blind so that God's work might be revealed in him.' That's the slightly misleading phrase in John's Gospel. What he's saying is that God's work can be revealed in anything. Resurrection always has the last word, if we'll let it.

So maybe where we stand in the story is with the disciples, asking the hard questions, eager to know more and to understand the mind of God. Someone once said that the average British Christian is as well prepared to meet an intelligent agnostic or atheist as a boy with a peashooter is to meet a tank. We have to stand alongside Jesus and question and read and discuss, and *think*.

But what about the blind man's parents? Where do they stand in the story? They're nearby and they don't want to get too involved. Which is odd, because they've been the ones who changed his nappies and calmed his blind frustrations, and guided his hand to the spoon and stayed with him at parties when he couldn't cope. But they've done their job in the main; he's of age, he's got his own friends now. And they can see trouble coming here. Get too close to this Galilean and you're out of the synagogue before you can say Leviticus. Discretion is the better part and all that.

That's a position many people take these days as well. Hanging around this Galilean is dangerous, even today. Indeed especially today. There have been more Christian martyrs killed for their faith in the last century than in any other century since Christ was born. And at a much more minor level, in style-conscious, cool Britannia it's very uncool to be passionate about Jesus, or indeed to be committed to anything – unless of course it's your football team, when you're allowed to jump around and yell like a five-year-old. But as for faith, well, we'd better keep it a little quiet. No point alarming the neighbours – they'd think we're fanatics. Moderation in all things.

Are we afraid of getting too deeply into faith ourselves and finding that we're mildly drunk on the beauty of God? And yet to be out of our depth is almost a defini-tion of faith. The fact is – Christ invites us not to be afraid, but to come closer and to trust his love.

So we've looked at the disciples, asking the hard ques-tions, and we've looked at the parents, wanting to keep their distance. Yet others, like the Pharisees, want to reject the power of the miracle entirely, and see themselves as His Majesty's Loyal Opposition. They'll always be there, drenching everything in cold water, always declaring that it's a sabbath so having a good time must be wrong, and the swing must be taken out of the budgie's cage in case it enjoys itself. Are we sometimes standing with this group as well?

But there's one place to stand that we haven't yet looked at – the position of the man born blind. He's right at the centre, facing Jesus with sightless eyes, waiting. And before we know it, Jesus is up to his old tricks again, taking spittle and dirt, mixing it up, and slapping the mud on to the man's eyes. And the great thing is this – it worked. He got his sight. As he said later, exasperated at the petty questions of the Pharisees, 'Look – one thing I know; once I was blind, and now I can see.'

And isn't that the best place to stand? 'Once I was blind and now I can see.' Bottom line; end of story, QED. What matters is that we're in a position in our Christian faith to be touched by Christ and to be changed. These other positions, these other places to stand around Christ, they're part of the journey most of us make – and in particular, those questions the disciples asked must always be a part of us. But what really matters is that we are *changed* by our faith, given our sight, transformed by the touch of Christ.

John Newton, the famous slave-trader turned hymn-writer, once said: 'I am not what I ought to be; I am not what I wish to be; I am not what I hope to be; but by the grace of God, I am not what I was.' It's the *experience* of Christ that ultimately matters, being in a position where Jesus can put the mud on our eyes, so that when we wash it away, we see the world afresh. The most effective cure for many of our religious ills would be to realize that *we are in God and that God is in us*.

Archbishop Deng was imprisoned and kept in solitary confinement in the Cultural Revolution in China. The Red Guards discovered his Bible and confiscated it, and slowly he found that his memory of much of the Bible was slipping away. But the central truths of the gospel became more and more luminous to him. 'I had it here,' he said, patting his breast, 'and they were the best years of my life.'

Someone with an experience is never at the mercy of someone with an argument. What we have to do as Christians is to place ourselves not on the edges of the story of Jesus but near the centre, where he can deal with us in whatever good and gracious way he wants. The experience of the living Christ is what ultimately matters, whether it be in the depths of prayer, in the mystery of worship, in the joys of love or the poignancy of sorrow; knowing the love of God in the living Christ is all that matters. At the end of the day there's just one place to stand in the story of Jesus. And that's as close to him as we can get.

For personal or group reflection

- Put yourself in the place of the disciples. What one question would you like to ask Jesus today?
  Now put yourself in the place of Jesus. How might he answer your question? (If doing this as a group, you could ask the group to work together on Jesus' answer.)
- Put yourself in the place of the parents of the blind man, not wanting to get too involved. What are the fears which stop us today from being open about our faith? What would Jesus say if we were honest enough

to tell him our fears? (Again the group could work on Jesus' answer.)

- Is there a blindness in us which needs healing? **Or** What was the main blindness from which Christ first set you free?
- How do you personally 'experience' Christ? Does that question make sense for you?

Further group activities

- Divide up into characters – Jesus, the blind man, the parents, the Pharisees – and get them to create a 'freeze-frame' picture of what it might have looked like when they were all together at one particular point in the story. How would the body language of the characters express their thoughts and feelings? The characters have to talk to each other to work out what was the likely effect on each of them. This discussion is the basis of the Bible study. The freeze-frame is then enacted, and maybe each person can leave the tableau for a moment and walk around it to see how each other person is represented.
- Brainstorm on to a large sheet of paper some of the ways that people characteristically experience the presence of Christ. Which of these are the most and least common? What do we say if someone doesn't recognize any of those categories as ringing true for them?
- How would you feel about this passage if you were physically blind?

For prayer

- Ask to be shown where your blind spots are.
- Pray for spiritual sight.
- Pray for those with sight problems and those who work with them, especially overseas where simple operations can restore sight and so re-create life for the whole family.

Recognizing God's footfall

THE TEN LEPERS: LUKE 17.11–19

What a life, what a living death those lepers had! There were ten of them, a little community of suffering, constantly shuffling around the countryside, keeping to the edges of the towns. Sometimes they were reduced to scavenging in bins round the back of the Pizza Parlour. They often had things thrown at them. The trouble was that they were so obvious. There was no disguising the stumps which used to be arms that held children and hands that caressed lovers. There was no disguising the diseased white skin and the red blotches and the painful breathing. But the worst pain was the rejection – always, total and absolute. 'Not here!' people said. 'Not in my back yard. Clear off!'

And then one morning as they came over the top of a dusty hill they saw in the distance a gaggle of young men and the unmistakeable figure of Jesus. They'd heard of him; who hadn't? But they never seemed to be in the same place at the same time as him. They kept their distance. Wary. But they called out for help nonetheless. Healers and magicians are worth a shout.

And this Jesus did the unthinkable; he started over towards them! It was so long since anybody had done that that they felt a quick rush of fear, but then they realized it was more a shiver of anticipation. This man had an air of something else – fresh from the desert in its purity and authority. They stopped, but still he came on. Almost defensively they called out for pity, like you do if you're a leper. But Jesus came right up to them and just when they thought this might be it – the Big Day, Serious Money, Major Food – he said something really naff. 'Go to church my friends, and show yourselves to the priests.'

'Oh thanks a bundle, Jesus! Yes of course the priests will love to see us! What they'll do is chase us out of their churches as fast as you can say AIDS!' That's what they felt, disappointment settling over them like a damp mist. But there was just something about that command they couldn't resist. Call them over-emotional, but there was a spooky sense of difference about this man. He said go, so they went.

As they were on the way it was young Samuel who noticed it first. 'Seth,' he said. 'What's happened to your skin?' They looked at each other in amazement and then they touched their pure skin, and they felt well-being glowing through their bodies, and they breathed deeply for the first time in years. They walked faster and then they ran and then they raced away, yelling and whooping and crying with delight.

But one leper, Seth, turned back. He was drawn to something else. There was another healing going on in him. He'd heard the voice of Another in the words of Jesus. He'd heard the rustle of God in the undergrowth, and he knew he had to go back, to where God was, in this man. He knew that God wasn't in a building in the town; he was here, before him. He recognized the foot-fall of God and knelt before him.

There's a deep desire in most of us to encounter the divine, something truly significant to sweep us off our bored and fretful feet. Many of us would love to recognize the presence of God much more often, to see his shadow on the landscape, to meet him over coffee with a friend, to stumble over the odd miracle just as it's happening, to bump into God in the midst of everyday life. And I suspect that people outside the churches are bumping into him rather more often than we think, but not wanting to associate that experience with the Church or with conventional Christian belief. Our culture is inescapably secular but people are inescapably religious. 'You can't keep a good God down!'

A feature writer in *The Big Issue* wrote of going to Aylesford Priory in Kent and finding himself sitting in a chapel which then got invaded by a group of strangers.

They were a pretty retro looking bunch – tank tops, Cornish pasty shoes and thick spectacles – and they were followed by a priest who proceeded to hand out prayer books. Now, under normal circumstances, I would take the piss, mercilessly. I've never been a great fan of established religion and have generally assumed that ardent practitioners are deluded, happy-clapping saddoes who make friends with God because they're too inept to do so with anyone on earth.

There was more than adequate material for a really biting satire. But there was one problem; I was deeply moved by the whole experience. No-one was more surprised than I, and no-one more determined not to be moved. I simply couldn't help it. There was a point in the service when everyone turned round to everyone else, shook hands, embraced and said 'Peace be to you'. It was brilliant. Uplifting. No doubt you'll be thinking 'What a jerk'. I'm in complete agreement. Yet I can't escape the fact that that service was one of the most spiritually liberating experiences I've ever had. It wasn't because of the words or the actions or the dogma. It certainly wasn't because of the free wine, which was gruesome. It was, I think, because of the underlying assumption of community. The sense that in this fragmented society of ours, where the spiritual is perpetually sidelined in favour of the material; where loving thy neighbour is something you do when thy neighbour's husband is out at work, that it's OK to be, well, soulful. I found to my eternal embarrassment that tears were pouring down my face. I had the sensation of being a child again. Where once I sniggered at the faithful, I now have a sneaking suspicion they might know more than I do.

People often find themselves surprised by God, but they don't expect to find him in church. That's a terrible indictment of the Church when our nation is spiritually hungry. Our churches should be power-houses of the Spirit, crackling with the vitality of God. They should be open, welcoming, ready for change and the wild excesses of God's glory, churches which are restless, exploratory, on their toes, searching for God's voice. Places where people say, 'Wow, what's going on here?'

I know that seems a tall order. But so was healing ten lepers that spring morning in the Palestinian countryside. Ten lepers were healed, but only one really got away, and entered the Kingdom. Only one recognized the source of his healing and turned back to him in surrender. In Britain, for every ten people, only one goes to church regularly. Only one gets away from the crowd. 'But were not all ten cleansed?' says Jesus. 'Where are the other nine?' The

Church has to go and find them! Many of them have bumped into God elsewhere but haven't given him a name, or turned back to him in surrender, or realized that the Church is where they might find him again.

We know that God is present everywhere, just under the surface, just round the corner, just out of sight (lest the glory burn us). But he's particularly present in the 'feast of fools' where Christians gather, and Christ is named, and together we knock on heaven's door.

For personal or group reflection

- When and where have you 'bumped into God' outside church recently?
- On a scale of 1 to 10, do you expect the church to be a place of stability or change? Is that OK?
- Is there any group of people you treat (subconsciously) as lepers?

Further group activities

- Who are society's lepers? Does the Church have a recognizably different approach to them?
- What would you say to the man at Aylesford Priory after his experience there?
- If you had to depict the Church in a colour or range or pattern of colours, what would it be, and why? Do this individually, then in threes, then together, exchanging insights.

For prayer

- Pray for anyone you know on the outside of the Church but spiritually searching.

- Pray for people with HIV/AIDS, those with disabilities, asylum seekers, the forgotten poor, and pray for the Church's ministry with such people both nationally and locally.
- Give thanks for your body and the miracle of its efficiency. Give thanks for your skin, your hands and feet, and the mighty miracle of the brain and the gift of human consciousness – which can recognize the presence and love of God himself.

All or nothing

PAYING TAXES TO CAESAR: LUKE 20.20–26

Let's imagine that scene in Luke 20. It's a familiar sce-
nario. In the red corner, the Pharisees and their groupies;
in the blue corner, Jesus and his young hopefuls, a mixture of recently resigned fishermen and tax inspectors.
Once again the Pharisees have come to get him. He's
making such a mess of their tidy religion. It was all so
neat before; you had 613 rules and regulations, and all
you had to do was enter at the right point and follow the
flow chart until you got to the right answer. But now
look at the rule book! All covered with crossings out and
corrections and question marks. What an unholy mess!

So what they'd got this time was a trick question.
Heads we win, tails Jesus loses. They thought it up the
previous night over a jar or two at the Sheep and Goats
down by the Damascus Gate. So in they came, all obse-
quious with wet palms and limp handshakes. 'Master,'
they said (nice one that; wrong-foot him; make him think
we're on his side), 'Master, we know you're an honest
and learned man who would have had an Oxford degree
if you'd been living somewhat later. And we know
you're not afraid of anyone, not nasty Mr Pilate from
Rome, and certainly not a group of slimy toads like us.
So tell us: should we pay taxes to Caesar or not? I mean,
we don't want to bother you, but we've just got this

self-assessment form and before we go to all this trouble we'd like to know what you think?'

That should do it, they thought. Nicely trapped. If he says 'Of course you should pay it', he'll be drummed out of the Brownies by every self-respecting nationalist in Jerusalem; if on the other hand he says 'Don't pay', he'll be walking straight into a charge of treason. 15–love.

But Jesus hadn't been born yesterday. 'Ratbags!' he says. Well, 'hypocrites' was the actual word; but neither description is very flattering. 'So here you are again! Why don't you give us all a break? But OK – let's have a look at a coin.' What's he up to? they thought. Nasty moment, this. The ground is slipping slightly. They handed him one of the special coins used for the temple tax, one with Caesar's smiling face on it. He's up to something, they thought. 15 all.

'So whose face is this then?' said Jesus. 'What's his name? Your starter for ten.' Definite trouble here; could be in for a rough ride. 15–30.

'Whose face? Well, Caesar's,' they replied, not quite knowing how they were being trussed up in a bag and hung out of an upstairs window, but feeling sure that that was what was happening. 15–40.

'OK,' said Jesus, 'that's fine. You give Caesar what belongs to him. But answer me this: what is it that belongs to God? What should you be giving him? The left-overs after Caesar's had his bit perhaps? Or the fag end of your time? How much of your life? Twenty per cent? Ten? Five? *Or maybe you've got it all wrong.*' Game, set and match.

What Jesus did was to expose the shallowness and wrong-headedness of their whole way of thinking. You can't say 'this bit belongs to the state and this bit belongs to God', as if God were a rather distant rival to Caesar. If God is God at all, the God of Abraham, Isaac and Jacob, the God of the darkness before creation, and the God of the blinding beauty of the world's dawn; if this is the God who breathes his life into us with every millisecond of our existence, without whom nothing exists for a moment, but with whom every miracle becomes possible; if this is the God we're dealing with, then everything, but everything, belongs to him – and Caesar gets his taxes *only with divine permission*.

So what do we do? If we accept Jesus' brilliant summary that everything belongs to God, including (by divine permission) our political life, then what do we do about it? Jesus was saying – it's all or nothing; your social and political existence, your life under Caesar, it all has to be lived for God.

So what shall we do? First, never accept the comment, 'The Church should stay out of politics.' Of course it should stay out of *party* politics, but the statement as it stands is plain heresy. The message of Jesus was about the kingship and universal sovereignty of God, not about the interior life of the soul divorced from the public life of the world. When did you last see a disembodied soul out of work, or a spirit blown up by a landmine? Desmond Tutu once said, 'When people suggest that religion and politics don't mix I'm puzzled about which Bible they are reading.'

Secondly, we can get involved in issues that go to the heart of what makes for a just society, the Kingdom that Jesus taught us to pray would come on earth, as it is in heaven. There's a parable about a factory in a little town in the middle of somewhere, and every day out of the factory gates would come people who were injured – with burns, broken arms, stress and more. So the local churches got together and put up an emergency clinic outside the factory gates. That helped, but the injured workers kept on coming, more and more of them.

So Rotary got involved, and the Lions, and lots of community groups, and they built a whole new doctors' surgery. This was splendid – but it did nothing to stop the tide of bruised and broken people who came out of the factory. So the Health Authority got involved and before long a wonderful new hospital was put up right there at the gates. But still they came, scores of them, day after day, more damaged than ever.

They were at a loss. They had a public meeting. What should they do now? Finally one man stood up. 'I know what we should do,' he said. 'We must go into that factory and we must demand to know what on earth it is that's going on there that's causing so much damage.'

And that's politics. Caring for causes, for reasons. There's an ethical imperative on the Christian to get involved in healing a broken world. The stakes are too high to ignore.

And thirdly, for some, the right response to the challenge of Jesus is to jump right in, personally, to the bruising arena of national or local politics, there to fight for the values of the Kingdom. Such people deserve real prayer and support. Our prayer, for them and with them, is part of the energy of change. The great (and fairly conservative) theologian Karl Barth said, 'To clasp the hands in prayer is the beginning of an uprising against the disorder of the world.' Pray for change, and for the politicians who seek it.

Whatever our action, let's remember it's a response to the call of Jesus, the man who had friends in low places, and sought their company, a man who was killed by a Roman politician and had a political charge nailed to his cross. A man who gave us the immortal challenge: 'Give to Caesar what belongs to Caesar (fair enough – he has a job to do), but give to God what belongs to God; which is nothing short of everything.'

Most of us have only just begun to glimpse the dimensions of that call. We've only just begun to call him Lord of our social and political existence. But our aim should be to work alongside anyone who's also concerned about the transformation and renewal of our world order. For that's what's ultimately at stake – the transformation of society and the coming of the Kingdom. 'Give to God what belongs to God.'

For personal or group reflection

* Are there areas of life you feel you haven't really tried to hand over to God?
* Where has your faith affected your social or political views?

Further group activities

* Read the quote from Desmond Tutu. Write down your immediate feelings and reactions. Then discuss together.
* Imagine a world where you had so much political power that you could make any changes you liked, but only if they were in line with God's priorities. What would be the first three changes you would make?
* Chart up together the marks and characteristics of the Kingdom of God. Are they the same as the marks of a just and peaceful society?

- Read the parable of the factory again. What are the 'factories' in our society that are doing that kind of damage? Is there anything we can do locally?

For prayer

'To clasp the hands in prayer is the beginning of an uprising against the disorder of the world.'

- What are the disorders that disturb you most? Pray for those people, great and small, who can do something about those problems. (You could try to find out more so that you can pray specifically and regularly.)
- Pray about the issues on the TV news or in the newspapers – even as you watch or read.

The eyes have it

JESUS' ENTRY INTO JERUSALEM: MATTHEW 21.1–11

Well, they wouldn't forget that day in a hurry. Passover was always special – the heaving crowds spilling down the Mount of Olives; bright-eyed children deliberately losing their parents, postcard sellers looking for a quick shekel with their faded pictures of the Temple, and pickpockets in and out as fast as you could say 'American Express'.

But this time there was an extra excitement in the air. The priests looked shiftier than usual, as if they were on the lookout for something. And the Roman soldiers were sweating away at the corner of every alley. Had they been tipped off? 'There could be trouble this time, Pilate. I know you think we Jews are all away with the fairies, but there's this Galilean upstart who really does seem a threat this time. People seem to be taken in by him. They hang around after his talks waiting for his autograph; they memorize everything he says and retell it down at the pub; they say they feel as if they've brushed shoulders with God! He's the talk of the town wherever you go – supermarkets and cocktail parties, tennis clubs and coffee shops. This year's big conversation piece. I tell you, Pilate, he's dangerous. As Caiaphas said only the other day – if it comes down to it, it's better for one man to die than for the whole nation to suffer. If he stirs up

71

the hot-heads, you Romans will only make mincemeat of us. So come on, do your stuff. Keep the peace. Take him down.'

But the crowds didn't know all that. That was politicians' talk. Out on the streets it was just hot, raw emotion. He was on his way! But who was he? They kept on asking that question. This was no crank, no religious hill-billy, even though he came from up-country where a new messiah popped his head over the parapet every year. But this Galilean was different – spoke straight from the heart with a clean, spare authority, pure as the desert. Went right through you, burning with truth.

And then there he was, sitting on a donkey – poor patient animal! And the crowds were jostling and the noise was deafening and there were palm leaves being torn from trees. But in the middle, that man, strangely still, as if in a cocoon of slow time. There was an odd sense of distance, a no-fly zone around him. And suddenly you could see why. The eyes. Some said they'd never forget the eyes. Dull with grief, focused somewhere else, somewhere not good, not good at all. The smile still played on his lips sometimes but the eyes and the soul were elsewhere.

And those who saw the eyes – well, they didn't want to laugh any more. They went home confused, troubled. And a chill passed over their soul.

One man, but two moods. Around him and within were both festival and fear; a holy bean-feast and a terrible foreboding; a triumphant entry and a desperate knowledge. And caught in the middle was a man whose sensitivities were stretched to breaking point this extraordinary morning. A huge longing for these glorious, foolish people to turn to their loving Father and find life. And an ache of the soul, past articulation, that they should give up trying to make God their own possession and just throw themselves recklessly into the huge high seas of grace. But it wouldn't work – and he knew it. It wouldn't work without the terrible victory of the cross coming first. And that was for him. That was where the donkey was taking him. No turning back.

I have a friend who was once awaiting a possible death sentence from the consultant. The rest of the world was getting ready for its Easter holidays, flying off to the sun, getting out the lawnmower, trying on the T-shirts. He waited. And he prayed. But before he could live again, he had to face the terror of his consultant's waiting room. Death or life? And yet his faith was like a rock, holy and strong, holy and immortal. He would celebrate the resurrection with profound joy, whatever came.

How is this done? Life and death, blessing and curse. How can you cope with both? Through every Christian century the answer has been the answer of Jesus – the cross. Only here can the great, tragic paradoxes of life be held together and woven into salvation. On that cross Jesus encountered the darkness full on, the darkness of a world that couldn't cope with his uncompromising goodness and so had to destroy him. Jesus took the full force of that darkness, absorbed it, drank the cup of black wine to the dregs, soaked up the pain that we've spilt all over history. He took it into the cosmic 'black hole' which is the cross, and saw it taken away by his Father.

Then – and only then – could he turn to the light and throw back the curtains of eternity. That's when he revealed the resurrection which has always been lying under the surface of every square inch of life. When Christ has defeated the darkness on its home ground, then the glorious possibilities of a world at one with its Lord start to operate. Only in places; only at times; but the deep engines of a new world are starting to hum. And our own darkness is thrown into that cosmic black hole too. Our rubbish goes into the same bin, our persistent failures, our meanness and selfishness, the unpleasant side of our mind that no-one sees. And we share the same victory. A Frenchman once became a naturalized Englishman and he was asked what he felt were the main differences. 'That's easy,' he said. 'Before, I lost the battle of Waterloo and afterwards I won it!' We share the victory of God, won on that cross. We don't win it again; we share what has already been done.

But that's to anticipate. On Palm Sunday Jesus was still only riding into all this, but by now he knew that the only way through this paradox of light and darkness was going to be a dark cross against a blood-red sky. And the eyes of Jesus told the story. They saw that some of the same people who greeted him with such a wild welcome were going to be the very people to bay for his blood in five days' time. Light and darkness, a paradox. And there could only be one answer – the cross.

The theologian Helmut Thielicke tells the story of a man who stood against the darkness of the Third Reich and in consequence was arrested and severely tortured. He was kept in solitary confinement, beaten and flogged for months, but he refused to give in and confess to anything. Eventually he was released without charge, worn out, undernourished, but unbroken in spirit and just as implacable in his opposition to the Nazis.

Two weeks after his release, however, he was found hanged in his attic, having committed suicide. People wondered what on earth could have caused him to do that, after all he'd gone through, but his best friends knew. He had made the terrible discovery that the person who had informed on him and delivered him to the Nazis had been his own son. What torture had not been able to do, betrayal by one he loved had finally achieved.

Betrayal by those he loved is what broke the heart of Jesus as he rode into Jerusalem that morning. These simple, misled people, loved by God from all eternity, loved in a way they couldn't even begin to imagine, were the very ones who would soon demand that Love be crucified. No wonder pain clouded his sight. No wonder those who saw his eyes would never forget.

We too face our greater and lesser paradoxes. The possibility of death when everyone else is getting ready for the summer. The struggle to hold on to our integrity in an organization that values only profit. The effort of holding a family together when inside we're falling apart. We know our own terror and joy, our own light and darkness. And only in the story of Jesus, and a cross and a resurrection, can we come to terms with these paradoxes. Only in the cross. But that cross is enough.

For personal or group reflection

- Have you ever experienced that simultaneous mixture of joy and pain which Jesus knew on Palm Sunday? How was it resolved?
- When has the cross helped you to make sense of life as you see it around you?
- Jesus demonstrated the way of sacrifice. Is there some sacrifice that you (or your church) have had to make, or perhaps are being called to make now?

Further group activity

- How might Jesus have entered Jerusalem (or your own town) today?
- How can the Christian Church today make an impact on the interested bystanders – the sorts of people who were in the crowd as Jesus rode into Jerusalem?
- Read the whole of Matthew chapter 21, preferably in a dramatized version. Keep five minutes' silence for reflection. Let people share their responses to the story.

For prayer

- Pray for specific sports-people, film stars and celebrities who receive the crowd's fickle and dangerous adulation, particularly for any you know of who are trying to live by their beliefs.
- Where have you felt betrayed? Pray for grace to forgive.
- Pray for any you know who have been betrayed, and for those who are suffering because of their faith.

Do you remember . . . ?

THE LAST SUPPER: MARK 14.12–26

Do you remember when you first rode a bike? Or when you poured orange juice down the telephone to get it to Granny in Scunthorpe? Do you remember the first time you went abroad and your father was so embarrassing with his French you practically passed out, or the first time you stole a kiss and didn't know what to do with your teeth? Do you remember when you got your O level or GCSE results, or when you first took communion?

Do you remember? It's important that we remember. It makes us what we are. And it certainly made the disciples what they were. The disciples remembered and remembered and remembered. And when they were in danger of not remembering they wrote it down so that they could keep on remembering. They had to remember Jesus, everything about him they possibly could. Particularly about that night, the night of the nightmare, when everything collapsed so horrendously you'd have thought the devil himself was let loose in the darkness.

It was an odd night from the start. The sunset was weird; the sky was blood red, and as dusk fell, an ominous waiting hovered over the city. The disciples hurried through the streets, feeling uneasy. Two of them had gone on ahead, to get to the supermarket before it shut for Passover and to find a donkey. Somehow Jesus had all this too well planned – it was a set-up, but who was in control?

Then there was the room. They would remember that. And a meal. They ate together every day, knew each other's likes and dislikes – Peter and his craving for goat's cheese, even if it smelt like his feet, and Thomas who never did like olives. But it was the atmosphere they remembered about this room. Like lead. Like thick darkness. Like the end of it all. Like the last night of God.

And then (do you remember?) he took the bread and the wine, like he'd done before, only this time, he took it painfully, as if it was hard to pick up, and he gave it to them. He looked each one of them straight in the eye as he did so. 'Do this,' he said, 'do this.' Remember. Do this. Remember. And their eyes were tired, and their heads were muzzy, but they remembered all right. Those eyes burning right through to the back of the brain – full of love and grief.

And there was that extraordinary incident over washing their feet, and Peter getting all worked up again. Will he never learn? And some heady teaching from Jesus, which John tried to scribble down on the corner of his serviette. And some dark words with Judas, who took a piece of bread from Jesus and then just slipped away into the night. And all the time the atmosphere was getting more and more tense, and the laughter more hollow, until there was virtually silence, and they ate, and thought their own thoughts.

Yes, they remembered all right. It was seared on their memories. John in particular used to think about that night again and again. And he wrote it all up, to try and make sense of it. He was always talking about it. He talked to the others when they came to see him and Mary in Ephesus; he talked to professors and peasants, anybody; he probably talked to his dog about it! He really wanted to *understand* that night. And to remember.

Memory makes us who we are. Talk to our children about being a Pritchard and you'll get a whole host of stories. Stories of camping in the rain in Wales, and family mutiny on Red Pike in the Lake District; stories of belligerent donkeys on Palm Sunday, and melting in the heat at Disney World. It's the same with a nation or a culture. A nation is made by its memories, shaped by them. And if it forgets its past it's like an actor forgetting his lines – suddenly he's nowhere, he's off the bus, he's lost his identity. Sometimes it seems as if western society has cultural amnesia about its Christian past. All it can do is try to reinvent itself every few years, with new values and a new image, because it's forgotten the story that shaped it.

Do you remember that story? One of the places where it's rehearsed and remembered most clearly is in the service of Holy Communion, celebrated week by week in a hundred thousand different ways around the world. What Jesus did at his last meal with his friends is vitally important to the Christian community. We're formed by our memory of this defining action, performed by Jesus to make us remember. He seemed to be trying to stamp the whole story on our memories.

It's like the story of the stranger who came to a tribe where the people all had hollow bamboo reeds with one hole in them, and when they blew down them they played just one note. But when the stranger came he made three holes in the reed, so that when he blew down it, he made a whole new series of notes – a melody. So they killed him. He was different. And we remember the story of our Stranger because of the music he made, but also because of the last meal before his death where he carved a new reed before their eyes, and gave it to them all to play.

Memory makes us who we are. Then we retell the memory to keep us on track and remind us of our task. 'Do this,' said Jesus after that famous last meal. Do this. Don't think this, discuss this, argue about this – just 'do this'. Don't watch it, smell it, wrap it in fancy clothes. Just 'do this'. And that's what we've tried to do, in season and out of season through a score of Christian centuries. It's been the sustaining mark of most Christian lives that regularly they have gathered with open hands to receive the life of Christ. Usually the context has been worship on Sunday morning, but sometimes the context has been surprising.

Buzz Aldrin was the second man on the moon, in that first Apollo XI spaceflight, and later he wrote this:

On the day of the moon landing we awoke at 5.30, Houston time. Neil Armstrong and I separated from Mike Collins in the command module. With only seconds worth of fuel left, we touched down at 3.30 p.m. Now was the moment for Communion. So I unstowed the elements in their flight packets. I put them and the scripture reading on the little table in front of the abort guidance system computer. Then I called back to Houston. 'Houston, this is Eagle. I'd like to request a few moments of silence. I'd like to invite each person listening in to contemplate for a moment the events of the last few hours and to give thanks in his own individual way.' For me, this meant taking Communion. I opened the little plastic packages which contained bread and wine. I poured wine into the chalice my parish had given me. In the one-sixth gravity of the moon, the wine curled slowly and gracefully up the cup. It was interesting to think that the very first liquid ever poured on the moon, and the first food eaten there, were consecrated elements.

Do you remember that first landing on the moon? Do you remember where you were when you heard of the death of Princess Diana? Do you remember your wedding service (no, in my case!). Do you remember your friends at Junior School, your first visit to hospital, going to the dentist? Do you remember? And do you remember Jesus, in that meal, washing feet, teaching his heart out, breaking bread, and then going out into the still, desperate night to take on the forces of darkness?

If we remember this Last Supper, we remember everything, for funnelled into this meal is the boundless life, the terrifying death, and the wild and wonderful resurrection of the young prince of glory. It's all there. And so Christians continue to break bread for the Church and pour wine for the world; to break bread for our sin and pour wine for our celebration; to break bread for each other and pour wine for the Kingdom. Do this, for Jesus' sake. And as we 'do this', we remember – we remember it all.

For personal or group reflection

- What things do you remember that have most shaped and defined your life? A clue – what stories, encounters, people, events do you find you repeat most often to people you have just met or don't know very well?

- What part of the Christian story, or the story of Jesus, do you honour most? What stories do you return to again and again?

Further group activities

- Brainstorm what words or phrases come to mind when the group thinks of Holy Communion. Are there any common groupings of ideas? Are there any surprising ideas? What are the three or four most important understandings of Communion this group has, and what might be missing?
- Make a list of the different sorts of time, place and style in which members of the group have experienced Holy Communion. How different did the meaning of the service seem in different places?
- What would make Communion at your church more meaningful? (Then tell the minister!)

For prayer

- Pray through your memories of the last day, asking help for others, forgiveness for yourself, or giving thanks.
- Pray that your next Communion service will 'catch fire' for you and for others. Pray for the regular leaders of the service, that they stay fresh and fully engaged.
- Take any hard memories you have to God and try to leave them there.

Judas – the man who lost the plot

JOHN 18.1–11

It was a quiet place – quite a favourite with Jesus, away from the crowds and the reporters, away from the tourist route and the postcards and the T-shirts (you know the sort of inscription: 'They went to Jerusalem and all I got was this lousy T-shirt'). This garden though, so quiet and cool, especially now, at night. There across the valley the lights of the city, brazen, unforgiving. The distant howl of a dog. A little animal scurries away through the sandy grass.

And Jesus was just getting up to rejoin the disciples, his face strained, as if he'd let something go, but at a huge cost. Then, as if choreographed, they all stop, frozen, listening. And in the middle distance the unmistakeable sound of urgent feet and the rustle of light armour, coming closer, up the hill from the little river Kidron. Now is the time, Jesus. Run! You have friends all over the city – they'll hide you. What are you waiting for? Go, now!

Into the clearing they come, as seen in a hundred medieval paintings. But this is for real – sharp steel and men with 'duty' stamped all over them. And breath that smells of fear, and tension crackling through the air. Jesus steps forward, his face a mask now, rock solid.

'Who do you want?' There's not much doubt about who it is, but they have to say it, to take responsibility for their actions. 'Who do you want?'

'Jesus the Nazarene,' they say.

'Well you've got him, that's me.' And then the earth seems to shake and before they know it they're on the ground, feeling stupid. What happened? The veil twitched, that's what happened; and divinity was on display, just for a moment.

But who's that other figure, bold and guilty at the same time as he stands there beside Jesus, cutting through this indecision, reaching towards Jesus to do – what? Surely not! Not a kiss! Judas! This is your friend, your master. Remember the long conversations, the fun on the road, the barbeques. Judas, what's got into you? You've really lost it!

So what was it that made him do it? The money? He was the treasurer after all. Perhaps he always had his hand in the till. And now it was the big one. Pay day. Jackpot. In the result he only got 30 pieces of silver. But what the Hades – it was a holiday in Tiberias. Nevertheless, that answer doesn't stack up. Why did he throw the money away a few hours later? Why hang himself? There's more to it than greed.

OK, so maybe he was set up. God needed a fall-guy. Somebody had to do the dirty work. Somebody had to be blamed in the Passion plays and the Sunday School lessons. But hold on. What kind of God are we suggesting here? A vindictive, arbitrary kind of God? 'You'll do, Judas – sorry about the injustice.' The cosmic puppeteer, pulling the strings at whim? No that won't do either; that's not the Father that Jesus loved so much.

So let's have a third try. Perhaps Judas just made a

horrendous mistake. Perhaps he thought Jesus was really the one who faithful Jews had been waiting for, the warrior king who would sweep out these infernal invaders and send them back to their fleshpots in Rome. But first, Jesus needed to be flushed out, helped to take centre stage. Until he did, the people wouldn't take to the streets. So he, Judas, had to help him. Let's precipitate a crisis, put him in danger and he'll have to raise the shout of revolt. Judas Iscariot – from the Latin 'sicarius', meaning dagger-bearer, knifer, razor-man, fanatic.

Judas and Jesus. Two men on completely different courses, and the tragedy is, Judas didn't even realize it. Those two courses collided in Gethsemane. Judas the misguided patriot; Jesus the servant Messiah. Judas just got it terribly wrong; he completely missed the point. Because Jesus didn't do a thing. To Judas' horror he just went along with it. No call to arms. No crowds pouring on to the streets to drive the Romans back to Caesarea. Jesus let himself be taken. He was on another track altogether. Judas had condemned this wonderful man to death. He saw it all now, and he was horrified. In a torment of grief he throws the money back at Annas and Caiaphas, but it's all too late. Only a lonely tree and a good strong rope will do now. And history's contempt.

Judas. The man who got it completely wrong.

So what's new? People always get it wrong. Well, what *is* new is that this is the Messiah he's got completely wrong, not just anybody. Nevertheless, we all do cheap cover versions of this kind of mistake. Which of us hasn't sometimes got it completely wrong? 'Do you know what I heard after church this morning? Of course I may have got it wrong but I don't think so . . .' 'Well I think he's up to no good; he's got a hidden motive.' 'No, no; that nice

Mr Attila the Hun, he wouldn't do that!' 'Well I've gone this far; I'm not going to turn back now, even if you're right.' 'Don't confuse me with the facts – we don't need all those lifeboats; the Titanic can't sink!' Sometimes, we just get it completely wrong.

Then there are only two answers and Judas picked the wrong one. He decided what he had done was so completely unacceptable he had to take his own life. The alternative answer was to throw himself on God's mercy. We don't know what would have happened then, but I have yet to meet the person who did that and got rejected. There seems to be no limit to God's loving forgiveness if only we'll set sail in it and experience the vast buoyancy of his grace. Nothing can sink us, if only we'll turn to him.

In 1979 the brutal dictator Somoza was overthrown in Nicaragua. In the new government the Interior Minister was Thomas Borge who had been tortured by Somoza's secret police and whose wife had been raped and then murdered. He was a committed Christian. Early on in his new job, Borge visited one of the prisons where former members of the police were being kept awaiting trial, and he recognized two of the men. 'Do you recognize me?' he asked. 'I'm Thomas Borge who you tortured and whose wife your colleagues raped and murdered.' They were aghast. 'Well,' said Borge, 'you're going to feel the full force of this revolution. I forgive you. Go, you're free.'

That forgiveness is an authentic echo of the astonishing grace and forgiveness of God himself. Too often people seem to think that God's forgiveness is like him leaning over the parapet of heaven, glaring down and saying: 'You're a wicked person, but because you've grovelled before me and pleaded guilty, I'll overlook it this time, but don't you dare do it again!' But it isn't like that at all. God longs to have us back and to remake the broken relationship. He's the father of the Prodigal, standing at the garden gate every day with his binoculars, scanning the horizon for his son.

Even if his name is Judas? we might ask. Well, and why not? If Judas had recognized that he had got it all terribly wrong and confessed his appalling mistake, would God have insisted he enter hell without passing 'Go' and without collecting £200? That doesn't seem to be what the cross was telling us about the inexhaustible love of the Father.

But we'll never know, because Judas took the quick way out and thereby placed himself in history as the unforgivable betrayer. So we're left, longing to tell him, 'Judas, even when you lost the plot, there was another way . . .'

And so there is for us.

For personal or group reflection

- Have you experienced God's forgiveness? What was that like?
- Jesus' death was for centuries blamed on the Jews and they suffered at the hands of Christians. Are you sure there aren't any anti-semitic feelings and responses in you?

Further group activities

- Set up a mini role-play based on Judas agreeing to betray Jesus (Matthew 26.14–16). You only need

Judas and two chief priests. Acting ability unnecessary! Then in the whole group, discuss Judas' motivation. Now read Matthew 27.1–10 and discuss the state of mind of Judas and the thinking of the chief priests.

- Think of those people who have committed the worst crimes recently or are most notorious. Are they forgivable? By whom? What does forgiveness mean in those situations?
- Have you come across stories of forgiveness (contemporary, historical, biblical) which have moved or impressed you? Share those with the group.

For prayer

- Is there anyone you haven't properly forgiven? Be honest! Ask for God's help to begin to forgive.
- Take to God anything you're getting completely wrong at the moment, and ask for forgiveness and wisdom.
- Pray for some of the people in the news recently, or of longer-term notoriety, who have committed major crimes and are now serving life sentences. Pray particularly for those who've committed the worst crimes and are most likely to feel they are 'beyond the pale'.

Simon of Cyrene – the man who lost his neutrality

MARK 15.16–22

He was just up from the country for a few days. He was having a short break to do a spot of shopping and a bit of sight-seeing, to catch up on the scandal and see his friends at the Club. Jerusalem was always a fascinating prospect for Simon. Everyone was a bit excitable here. Cyrene was much more peaceful, in spite of all the Jews who'd settled there to get some of the rich pickings of North Africa. But people were always plotting something new here in Jerusalem, a minor revolt perhaps or how to break the new traffic laws round the Temple precincts. All good clean fun – unless the Romans took exception and went in for another orgy of crucifixions *pour encourager les autres*, as those people from Gaul would say later.

So here he was, Simon the unknown, sauntering along the narrow streets, enjoying the markets and the colour and the atmosphere, when he came across something of a crowd. 'What's up?' he thought. 'Chariot lost a wheel? Bit of a punch-up over a deviant interpretation of Jewish Law?' He pushed his way to the front. Simon was quite a commanding figure; that's probably what got him noticed, that and his swarthy colour.

He quickly saw what was happening. Another crucifixion. Another poor wretch who'd put his foot over
some line or other. There he was. Blood and sweat all
over his face. Hardly dressed – just enough to humiliate,
and to show the awful red scars, weeping with pain. Why
did these Romans have to be so cruel?

Then all of a sudden it happened. The man just keeled
over and that great big crossbeam rolled off his back and
landed right in front of Simon. He could see the blood-
stains on the dark wood. And then this soldier – over-fed
and sweating heavily under his uniform – he just fixed
Simon in a no-nonsense glare, which said: 'You're in the
frame, laddie; don't even think about another way of
spending this afternoon.' And he didn't. He was pulled
out of the crowd, and he bent to pick up the crossbeam.

And down there, amongst the dirt and debris of that
Jerusalem street, his life changed for ever. He looked
straight into the face of Jesus, from nine inches. People
asked him afterwards – indeed for the rest of his life –
what was it like? What did you see there? And all he
could say was: 'I saw God. Or something very like him. I
was thunderstruck. I saw Love in agony; I saw the beauty
and the pain and the madness of it all, and I desperately
wanted to do something, anything, to relieve the pain of
this crippled angel. I seized the beam and scrambled to
my feet, as quickly as the weight of that outrageous lump
of wood allowed. And then like a man possessed I
dragged myself up that terrible hill.

'It felt as if there was something supernatural about
that crossbeam; its weight wasn't just to be measured in
pounds; it seemed to be possessed by demons, to be alive
with malice and hate. I shudder to think of it even now.
But we got there and I collapsed to the ground, too

terrified to watch as they hammered my new Lord to that demonic cross. I don't know what I did after that. I think I just wandered around Jerusalem in a daze for hours. But I would do it again, any time, anywhere, just to take an inch of suffering off his back.'

Simon – the man who lost his neutrality; the man who came out of the shadows; the man who took up a cross for the rest of his life. What does it take to get us out of the crowd, off the sidelines, out of the shadows? What will pull us out of the massed ranks of the 1st Battalion Innocent Bystanders?

A few years ago I was a vicar in Taunton and one Good Friday we organized a large-scale Passion play through the town, using familiar landmarks like the town hall steps for the encounter with Pilate, and the market square for the crucifixion itself. I wasn't acting; I was in the crowd, and I remember standing by the road from the crucifixion to the church, amongst the thousand or so spectators. I was content. We'd done what we intended; we'd brought the town centre to a standstill. I stood at the roadside waiting for the dead body of my curate to be carried past shoulder high.

And then suddenly I found myself being seized, and pulled out of the crowd. I was being thrust into the heart of the action, to help carry the dead Christ down the long road into the church. He was heavy, awkward. There were hundreds of eyes on us. Would I drop him? And this was the body I had watched throughout the Passion – from a safe distance, watching the clean, domesticated violence. But now it was flesh and awkward bone, weight and sweat and a total invasion of my space. But I was in it. No longer a spectator. And it made all the difference in the world.

What does it take to get us out of the crowd and on to the field of play? What does it take to make us lose our neutrality and get committed? The trouble is that life has become something of a spectator sport for us, an exercise in virtual reality. We can sit by our TV and computer screens and travel all over the world – inspect the ceiling of the Sistine Chapel, explore the Pyramids in Egypt, listen to a speech by Winston Churchill. Why 'do it' when you can fake it? Why get involved when you can watch?

That approach has affected every part of our national life. Our culture is one of cool observation, not passionate commitment. And yet those figures we see on our TV screens are bleeding. They're not just news entertainment; they're broken children of God. Society needs people who will get their hands dirty, go the extra mile, and do the unglamorous work of invisible care. And up at the front of the queue should be the people of God. Others, wonderfully, will be there too, often shaming Christians by their compassion. But Christians, at any rate, should have the motivation to come off the sidelines and into the action, whether it be by working with asylum seekers or homeless people, by listening to the bereaved, or by letter-writing for Amnesty. Christians, of all people, can't be spectators because they celebrate a God who came into the heart of human experience and all its need, and who chose the way of commitment and sacrifice – even to the point of death.

Those of us who dare to call ourselves Christians ought to get drawn out of the stands and on to the field of play. The Christian life has to be lived out in small particulars. If we're in the thick of life's hard places, loving consistently and still retaining the grace and joy of the gospel, then we won't need to invite people to come to church;

people will be scrabbling at the door to come in and see what it is we've found.

Simon of Cyrene lost his neutrality that day, and found a kingdom. And so it still is today for all those who come out of the shadows and follow Christ.

For personal or group reflection

- As Jesus hangs on the cross, where do you place yourself in the scene, and why?
- What do you do differently in your commitment to the needs of others that you might not do if you weren't a Christian?
- Who might need your help in carrying their cross at the moment?

Further group activities

- Try painting a corporate picture of the scene with Simon picking up that cross. Each person is asked to offer one detail to the scene as they imagine it. Keep going round the group until as full a picture as possible has emerged. Discuss the varied mental pictures we carry of biblical scenes.
- Members of the group can be asked to share any experience of God's call to 'come out of the shadows'.
- What difference would it make to the life and health of the community if your local church was not there? What difference would it make if *individual Christians* were not there?

For prayer

- Imagine you have been carrying the cross for Jesus. As you hand it back at Golgotha, what do you want to say to him? What does he say to you?
- Pray for some of the 'innocent bystanders' you see around the edge of faith and of your church. Pray for them to come out of the shadows.
- Give thanks for those who at times pick up your cross for you.

Jesus – the man who nearly lost God

MARK 15.27–39

It's hard to enter the mind of a dying man. You can get just so close and then it begins to feel blasphemous. 'What did it feel like, Jesus?'; 'What hurt most?'; 'Would you do anything differently if you could do it again?'

But that's awful. This isn't a time for reporters' questions. This is a time of extraordinary intimacy between Jesus and his Father. We're eavesdropping on the pain at the heart of God. And what do we hear? We hear a man who nearly lost God. More seriously, we hear *the* Man, nearly losing God. As he hangs halfway between heaven and earth we hear those terrible, horrific words: 'My God, my God, why have you forsaken me?' A chill seizes our soul. This is Jesus, losing hold of God. If that can happen to him, what hope for us?

Good Friday is a bewildering day. A worldwide survey in 1995 found that while 88 per cent of people recognized the logo for McDonalds, only 54 per cent knew what the cross symbolized. On the other hand, for those who understand and can enter the darkness of this day, it's nothing short of terrifying. Some people can't stand Good Friday; they want it out of the way as soon as possible; it's the worst day of the year. Outside in the streets of our towns and villages most people are just getting on with life, working, shopping, cleaning the car, jetting off for an early holiday. While we in church are contemplating nothing less than spiritual chaos. Everything is collapsing; anarchy is let loose upon the world. God the Holy Trinity is going into meltdown.

So what's going on here? How can we make sense of this catastrophic event? Look at it this way. (And there are other ways; the cross is too rich and kaleidoscopic to be reduced to one explanation. But try it this way.) God has been calling his foolish people back for as long as he and they can remember. His voice is hoarse with calling them back to their covenant with him. The kings, the priests, the prophets – they've all tried; some harder than others. But now the faithful people of God, the faithful remnant, are really reduced to just this one man. There's only one fully faithful man left, and now he's strung up on a cross. All the hopes of God rest on this one faithful person, the personification of Israel as she was meant to be. But now even this last final thread is about to break because the darkness of the world is overwhelming even Jesus and he experiences utter dereliction. 'My God, my God, why have you left me, deserted me, abandoned me, why, why?' Why have you left your people to madness and fear and anarchy? It's the darkest moment in the history of the world.

Of course people try and justify this enigmatic and appalling question. He's just quoting from Psalm 22, they say, like any good Jew would do in such an extremity. The psalm ends in hope, they say, so it's really a cry of confidence. But that's trying to wriggle off the hook! Here is the light of the world, the light that the darkness has never put out, being put out! This is really bad news.

But it's absolutely unavoidable. There's no other way left. It's the cross or nothing. The cross will obliterate everything Jesus stood for, but only in this way will he defeat evil on its own ground. If evil is to be defeated, it will have to do its worst, claim its victim – and still lose. So Jesus took into himself all the evil and hatred, the anger and violence, the deceit, pride, greed – whatever you like; and he absorbed it, soaked it up, like a sponge drawing into himself everything we've spilt and wasted. And then when he had mopped up the last dregs of the misery of humankind, he squeezed it out into the care of his Father. It drained out from him into the Father's heart. But with that supreme effort, he had nothing left. He could only die. 'It is finished.'

When one of our daughters was small she would sometimes get beside herself with rage. And since it's hard to reason with a volcano all we could do very often was to hold out our arms and draw this furious little body into our embrace. The fists and arms would flail against us, and we would just have to absorb the attack until eventually the little body flopped, all passion spent. The anger had drained away. She was free to live again. In some such way the cross absorbs our darkness and lets us go free.

So how does all this help? What can we do with this picture of Jesus hanging there, and this explanation of what it was all about? Well, firstly, now we know where God is to be found – he's on a cross. And when we encounter raw suffering in a hurting world it's important to know where God is. A young mother dying of cancer – where is God in all this? A child cut down by a speeding car – where on earth or in hell is God? So much faith has been shipwrecked by suffering, just at the time when people need God most. Where is God? The answer is – hanging on the same cross as the mother and the child.

One of the most powerful illustrations of this comes in Elie Wiesel's book *Night*, in which he writes about his experiences in a Nazi concentration camp.

The SS seemed more preoccupied, more disturbed than usual. To hang a young boy in front of thousands of spectators was no light matter. The head of the camp read the verdict. All eyes were on the child. He was lividly pale, almost calm, biting his lips. The three victims mounted together onto the chairs. The three necks were placed at the same moment within the nooses. 'Long live liberty' cried the two adults. But the child was silent. 'Where is God? Where is he?' someone behind me asked. The three chairs tipped over. Total silence throughout the camp. On the horizon the sun was setting. We were weeping. Then the march past began. The two adults were no longer alive. [. . .] But the third rope was still moving; being so light, the child was still alive. [. . .] Behind me I heard the same man asking: 'Where is God now?' And I heard a voice within me answer him: 'Where is he? Here he is – hanging here on this gallows . . .'

Now we know where God is often to be found in this world – he's on a cross, suffering alongside us.

A second way we can be affected by the terrible image of Christ hanging on the cross is this: now we know our responsibility in facing evil. When confronted with evil in any of its myriad expressions, our task is to take into ourselves, almost to inhale, the victory of the cross and thereby to hold the line against evil, to refuse to let it pass, to give it no more room for manoeuvre in ourselves or in this bit of the world we can influence. But we can't do this on our own resources; we have first to appropriate the victory of the cross, to live in it and it in us, to live in a different country with a different strength.

Evil is still rampant in our own experience and throughout our fractured world. The cross hasn't swept away all the rubbish in one go. But in potential it has. The final victory isn't in doubt. D-Day has passed and it's VE Day we await. Until then, we must hold the line with the power of love, and advance inch by inch against the forces of destruction.

So as we look at Jesus on his cross, now we know where God is often to be found; and now we know what we have to do in facing evil. And a third thing – now we know something of the strange fruit of suffering. Suffering had always looked as if it was nothing but bleak tragedy. Now we know that through suffering can come hard, unsought, but undeniable fragments of a new life. The darkness of my stress-induced illness some years ago taught me more than I can say. The loss of his job gave a friend of mine the opportunity to explore a whole new life. The departure of a husband brought another friend of mine to an exciting faith.

Suffering has this strange potential. Someone once wrote: 'In Italy for thirty years under the Borgias they had warfare, terror, murder, bloodshed – but they produced Michelangelo, Leonardo da Vinci and the Renaissance. In Switzerland they had peace, brotherly love and five hundred years of democracy, and what did that produce? . . . The cuckoo clock.' Suffering may produce a strange fruit. It's called redemption.

One last point. The only thing we have to offer people in pain is the cross. It's no good offering false promises or impossible cures. 'You'll get over it soon.' 'My uncle George had this and he was soon back in the garden.' 'We're all praying for a miracle, you know.' Yes we can offer a miracle, but only the miracle of the cross, of a God who enters our suffering, knows it, shares it, takes it into himself and promises never, ever, to leave us. The miracle is of a crucified God who takes responsibility for the suffering of the world he has given us, and sometimes, just sometimes, that love is able to bring about remarkable, even 'miraculous', change. But the most important thing is that he'll stay with us to the very end of any wounding road we're on, and give us always our daily bread – of love, strength, patience and more.

Jesus – the man who nearly lost God. But didn't.

For personal or group reflection

- How would you most like to spend Good Friday?
- When have you experienced the full assault of suffering, and what resources did you have to help you cope?
- Has the cross and the sight of a crucified God helped you to face suffering?

Further group activities

- Perhaps in threes, share experiences of when you nearly lost God – and what happened next.
- Take today's newspaper and spend time, in small groups, marking with a felt pen the situations of suffering reported in it. How would you answer someone who said about each situation: 'So what's your God got to say about that then?'

- Divide into small groups and look at one each of the following texts, and be prepared to report back on what light is shed on the problem of suffering from that passage. Genesis 3; Job 40.1–9; Luke 13.1–5; Luke 23.32–46; Romans 8.31–39; Revelation 21.1–7.

For prayer

- Take three candles or nightlights. Light one and pray for a situation in the world which troubles you. Light a second and pray for someone you know going through a hard time. Light a third and pray for yourself and any problem or pain you are experiencing now.
- Look at Jesus on the cross. Stay there; keep looking, even when you want to turn away; see the scene; watch the people; listen to the crowd; smell the fear. Edge nearer to the cross. Look at that broken figure. If you have anything to say to him, do so now.

Joseph of Arimathea – the man who lost his grave

LUKE 23.50–56

He was a man of principle – that was the first thing you noticed about Joseph of Arimathea. He was a member of the Jewish Council, but he wasn't in love with it – or with himself. He knew the ropes, he knew the politics, but he wasn't seduced; he hadn't lost his values or his ideals. And he could tell a political stitch-up when he saw it. That's what had gone on with this young charismatic teacher – a stitch-up, for pretty sordid political reasons. We have to keep the Romans sweet, they said; no hero figures, no revolutionaries, no cult evangelists. And what about us, they said? What about our position as the recognized leaders and teachers of what's kosher and what isn't? He's a dangerous little upstart, this Jesus; we have to take him down a peg or two (or rather, up – on a cross), before he gets too big for his sandals.

But Joseph knew this was wrong. So he just said, 'No. What you're doing is ridiculous. Grow up and don't be so bumptious. He's a good Jewish boy with something rather special to offer. I'm not quite sure what it is, but it's from the Lord (may his name be praised).' But they weren't listening of course. Never did when it was Joseph. Off on another of his moral crusades, they said. Against stoning for adultery one day; on about fairly traded coffee the next. Now it was loonies from Galilee he wanted to protect.

So he lost. And so did the young teacher. It was an awful Roman barbarity this crucifixion. Broken men dying by inches, their eerie groans going on for days on occasions. And sometimes there were scores or even hundreds of them at the same time. To teach us a lesson, thought Joseph, but they don't have a clue, these Romans. The chosen people don't just roll over for some self-proclaimed demi-god in Rome. 'We'll be back,' he said.

But with this Jesus he was damned if he was going to give up his integrity. What he could do instead was give up his grave. The more he thought about it, the more he knew it had to be done. He had this nice little plot of land, and a nicely prepared grave – enough space, enough dignity. Jesus would have it. At least one member of the Council would play fair. And what *was* it about this man? Why *did* he get under the skin?

So he went over to Mary, the young man's mother, where she stood, sobbing quietly some yards from that horrendous cross. He approached quietly, apologetically – after all it was his colleagues who were doing this to her son. And he offered his grave and his help, and the poor distraught woman accepted it, bewildered and relieved. He even summoned up the courage to see Pilate and ask for the body, and that pathetic bully seemed almost too anxious to get rid of the whole business. He gave permission without even a bribe.

So Joseph went back to Golgotha, and to that mis-shapen Messiah, and gently, gently did the deed. He had the crossbeam lowered, withdrew the terrible nails from the torn flesh, carried the body carefully in a cloth to the tomb, wiped the worst of the blood away with ointment, and left the body there in the grave, for better attention after the sabbath. Joseph's servants rolled the huge stone in the groove across the mouth of the tomb. Gone. All gone. In a borrowed grave.

What is it that Joseph had done? He'd given up his grave, certainly. But hadn't he also *created space for the resurrection*? Hadn't he given God room to perform the miracle that would change the world? Just as God needed Mary to give him space in her womb to enter this life – he needed her permission – so he needed someone to make space for the resurrection. Good old Joseph! What a gift he gave, unknowingly, to the Lord of Hosts.

And in a sense that's all we can do too – create space for God to act, space in our lives, space in our church, space in our society. We can't force God to act, in resurrection or indeed in anything. God isn't our puppet, our genie of the lamp to be summoned up on demand. All we can do is provide the space. We can no more force God's hand than force the daffodils to grow in spring. God grows in his own way, and sometimes he grows out of strange places.

In the Nuremberg war crimes trials a witness appeared who'd lived for a time in a grave in a Jewish cemetery. There was nowhere else for him and many others after they'd escaped the gas chamber. In a grave nearby a young woman had given birth to a child, assisted by an 80-year-old gravedigger. When the new-born baby gave his first cry the old man exclaimed: 'Great God, have you finally sent the Messiah to us? For who else than the Messiah himself can be born in a grave?'

The risen Christ, in actuality, was born in a grave, and the only role Joseph had at that time was to make space for it to happen. It's all we can do now – make space in our lives for Christ to be raised. Raised by God, in his own time and in his own way. But we're not very good at making space in our lives for anything other than what we want to happen. We prefer to fill our lives, not empty them, to make sure they're full of distractions and entertainment. When we come into the house the first thing we do is turn on the radio. When we have a spare moment we find a hundred things to fill it with. Our lives are often crammed full of our own trivia.

A monk was once visited by a man who wanted to learn about prayer, but instead of listening to the man of prayer the visitor kept talking about all his own ideas. After a while the monk made a pot of tea and he poured it into his visitor's cup until it was full. Then he went on pouring and pouring until the tea was all over the saucer and the table and starting to go on to the floor.

Eventually the visitor couldn't restrain himself any longer. 'Don't you see?' he said. 'It's full. You can't get any more in.'

'Exactly,' said the monk. 'Just like you. You're so full of your own ideas there's no room for anything else. How do you expect to learn about prayer unless you have space?'

How indeed? And how can we receive either the grace of prayer or the miracle of Christ's risen life within us, if we don't make space for him? That's all we're able to do, but in fact it's everything. We can supply the grave in which the Lord is laid. And wait. Resurrection is God's work, not ours. 'We do not presume . . .'

As Joseph of Arimathea was deciding what to do, the Lord of glory had almost died; the light had almost gone out. Jesus had completed his cosmic task, and turned toward sister Death. And ever since, that next day, Saturday, has been a day of holy grief, a day of sacred silence. The worst day of the year in a sense, because it's the only day when, in the Christian story, Christ is not alive.

But listen. Even as we watch that 'poor, bare, forked thing', as he closes his eyes for the last time, do we not hear in the distance, beyond the mountains, the growing roar of resurrection?

For personal or group reflection

- How much space is there in your life – quiet space, Godspace, space for the unexpected?
- Is there an area of your life where you can feel the excitement of something new getting under way? How can you encourage that new birth?
- Is there some space in your life which you could give to someone else who could use it well?

Further group activities

- Decide on a one-line statement which each of the following characters might have said about Joseph's offer of his new grave: Mary the mother, Mary Magdalene, John, Caiaphas, Pilate, a Roman soldier, a member of the crowd. For example, Mary the mother might say about Joseph: 'He's a good man with a conscience and he recognizes a mother's pain.' But Caiaphas might say . . . what?
- Light a candle. Say there will be ten minutes' silence together. Say slowly the words: 'Be still, and know that I am God.' After ten minutes invite people to talk

about what the silence meant to them, how they felt about it, and what happened.

For prayer

- Shape your joined hands in your lap as a cup. Ask God to give you whatever he wants. And then keep silence, only repeating or rephrasing the request when necessary.
- Pray for any Mary you know in bereavement, or any Joseph of Arimathea, wanting to find God.

The women at the tomb – look for the living among the living

LUKE 24.1–12

It was a grim little procession that set out for the garden. Mary, Joanna, Mary Magdalene, with their sad little bundles of spices, moved quietly through the grey streets in the early dawn. There wasn't much to say. They knew what they had to do; anointing bodies was a familiar task. But not this body! Everything in them rose up in rebellion at having to anoint *this* body. This was a body they could only associate with life, not death. In their mind's eye they saw him striding confidently along the dusty roads of Galilee with the sun shining and heaven in the air. They saw him kneeling tenderly with a sick child and pouring his love into the child until she smiled with health. They saw him riding into Jerusalem on that funny little donkey, and everyone going wild with excitement.

So this extraordinary task of anointing his dead body was completely absurd. It made no sense. It was a collapse of rationality. And it was also the death of all the hopes and anticipations which had risen up within them, the thrill of the chase trying to keep up with Jesus' ideas, the delight of learning new things about themselves and about God, the excitement of hearing about the Kingdom of God coming over the horizon. But now it was over. It was all over.

So they wound their way through the tired streets with yesterday's debris still on the ground. They picked their way past the silent guards, half-asleep at the gates, and then they were within sight of the garden and the tomb, and bleak despair swept over them again. But they found their pace increasing, a deep urge within them to get to the tomb. What was that about? What was that shimmering sensation in the air?

They turned a corner and froze, as if winded. The tomb was wide open! After a few moments they crept slowly forward again, feeling dizzy with anticipation, feeling as if their hearts were about to burst. Mary Magdalene led the way in. Empty! What? How? Who? Thoughts tumbled over each other and careered wildly into the abyss. This was crazy!

And then, even as they gazed at the strips of grave cloth lying empty and bereft, like a glove from which the hand had gone, they were aware of a presence. Behind them, silhouetted against the doorway of the grave with the light of the dawn behind them, were two men they didn't recognize. Had they been outside all along? They hadn't seen them. And then one of them spoke, and said those words which would echo inside them for the rest of their lives: 'Why do you look for the living among the dead? He is not here; he is risen.'

Terror and joy exploded through them. The living, the living? Jesus – among the living? They teetered on the edge of madness. They'd seen him dead, dead as a corpse can be, white, ghastly, without breath, without life. Taken down from a cross; put in a tomb. Dead. Definitely dead.

And now? 'Why do you look for the living among the

dead?' These men seem to be saying, almost mischievously, 'Shall we take a look? See if you can see him. Bet you can't!' He's alive, they're saying. Alive! And all of life is ablaze with glory.

Even then, though their minds were in total turbulence, they began to remember – fragments of conversations, things he'd said that they'd filed away under 'pending' or 'random remarks of a spiritual genius'. Had he suspected something might happen? And then they were ejected from the tomb by sheer joy, and Luke says 'they returned to the disciples'. Surely they didn't just 'return'! They flew, they danced, they somersaulted! When people fall in love or receive wonderful news they don't go and put out the dustbins or clean the bathroom or 'return'; they sing and dance and go slightly mad. So back they surged to the disciples, and they told their story.

And ever since, that story has been told in a thousand million ways, and the reverberations of that explosion on Easter morning are still being felt in every corner of the world. 'Why do you look for the living among the dead?' Why do *we* look for the living among the dead? Why are we so slow to believe, so grudging about the resurrection? Why do we go grubbing around in the graveyard of our tired ideas and experiences, looking for Christ in the gloom and doubt of our half-belief? He is not here; he is risen.

Janani Luwum was Archbishop of Uganda when Idi Amin was President. He suffered the fate of many good people at that time; he was killed. Thousands of people gathered on the hill called Namirembe in Nairobi, devastated at the news. But they had no body to mourn with because the Government wouldn't give it back. The people just stood around, lost.

Then the old Archbishop, Erica Sabiti, came out and began to read the story of the resurrection. He reached the part where the two strangers say to the women: 'Why do you look for the living among the dead?' and spontaneously a song of praise started up all around the hillside. 'Glory, glory, hallelujah.' Everyone began to realize what the passage meant. Janani Luwum was not a corpse in a government mortuary; he was a child of God safe in the presence of a living Lord. Glory, glory, hallelujah.

On Easter Day Jesus issues a challenge: 'Who says I'm dead? Why do you go on looking for me among the dead?' Because the places we'll find him are those where death is dying, where grey is turning to colour, and green shoots are breaking through concrete, where the blind are recovering their sight, and the oppressed are going free. The characteristic activity of the risen Christ is to bring people and places to life. People will know that Christ is alive, therefore, when they see transformation taking place before their eyes and want a piece of the action. And that's a straight challenge to us, direct from the risen Christ. How are we demonstrating that Christ is alive?

'Who says I'm dead?' Well, sadly, the Church itself often seems to say it. In the west, there's often been more fear than faith in our Christianity, more gloom than joy. No wonder people have looked elsewhere for life and meaning. A young man, genuinely searching for God, once went to church for a considerable period but then stopped. The reason was, he said, that week by week he would come out from the experience not feeling that life had been affirmed, but that somehow life had been made smaller and he had been diminished. That's a tragic indictment of the church. Those Christians probably

111

never even laughed in church. How can you be fully human and fully alive without laughing?

The trouble is we've been preoccupied with sin and death and what they did to Jesus, rather than being preoccupied with Jesus and what he did with sin and death. The Church has to get back to the risen Christ; its ministry has to be shaped by the resurrection. We need to be an Easter people with hallelujah as our song, and (as Gerard Manley Hopkins wrote) to let Christ 'easter' in us. We need to affirm with complete confidence that Christ was raised from the dead, and that here was the dawn of a new world which we can share now in the hugger-mugger of everyday life. And if we experience that for ourselves, and demonstrate that risen life in how we live, maybe it will begin to rub off on others. Maybe we'll all be challenged to stop and think, to listen to the silent music in our own hearts, and notice the occasional shafts of light from another world.

Why do we look for the living among the dead? Christ is found where there's life, because what he's doing all the time is bringing people and places to life with his loving touch. Our task is to share the resurrection, to live it and show it, so that people will know that great resurrection truth: the living One is among the living, not the dead.

For personal or group reflection

- Are you an Easter person or a Good Friday person?
- When and how did the resurrection first impinge on your life?
- When have you 'caught sight' of the risen Lord?

Further group activities

- Individually jot down words which complete the sentence: 'If Christ is alive, then I . . .' Do that a few times, building up a list. Then in the group on a flip chart draw up a corporate list, discussing your shared experience as you go.
- The resurrection is a truth beyond words. What pieces of music express something of the resurrection for members of the group? If possible the group could be asked beforehand to bring such pieces of music to play on tape or CD during the session.
- What persuades you of the truth of the resurrection? Could anything dissuade you?

For prayer

- Let the words 'Jesus Christ is risen today' roll around in your mind. Chew the words for as long as you like; suck the goodness out of them; let their meaning seep through your whole being. And give thanks.
- Light a candle for anyone who is struggling in the dark in his or her life at present. 'Lord, I light this candle for . . . Give him your light, and help him to see light.'
- Pray for greater confidence in your faith or the faith of others, because Christ is risen and is with us for ever.

Thomas – the man who wanted everything

JOHN 20.24–29

The problem was he hadn't been there the first time. Thomas had been out in the streets somewhere, wandering around in a daze. He'd done that a lot since Friday, since the killing. Said he needed space to think. So when Jesus broke into their lives again in the Upper Room, leaving them gasping for breath and struggling to stay sane, Thomas missed him.

Which was a shame, because Thomas above all needed to see him, stare at him, talk to him. Thomas never seemed to be your actual 100 per cent believer. Often when they were in Galilee you could see that look coming into his eye which seemed to say, 'OK Jesus, could you just do that again, only slowly this time, so we can see how you did it?' So when Thomas came through the door that evening and the others grabbed him and started gabbling on about Jesus having been there with them, it wasn't surprising that Thomas was less than impressed.

'OK guys. You've been cooped up here long enough. You're getting yourselves all hyped up. I understand what you're saying but forget it. Unless I see him, and the holes where those terrible nails went in, and that appalling wound in his side, I'm afraid you've got to count me out on this one.' For the rest of the evening there was rather an awkward atmosphere: the other disciples talked avidly among themselves, while Thomas just got on with the crossword.

In fact the whole week was weird. Days went by and nothing happened again. Even the disciples began to wonder if they'd just imagined it. When they talked about it Thomas began to look a little smug. They began to go out a bit more to get a bit of fresh air and to do some shopping – but always carefully, at dusk, and looking behind them. If they were recognized as friends of the crucified Galilean they might still be in a load of trouble.

It was Sunday night when it happened. They were sitting around, with debris from the take-away still on the table and sections of the *Jerusalem Times* strewn about the floor. The door was still locked. Later they would swear to that – Peter had the key and he was very careful. But suddenly the atmosphere became electric; voices stopped in mid-sentence; hearts started thumping; something astonishing had happened. And then they saw him. Unmistakeably him, though not – what? – not *quite* the Jesus they remembered. More vivid, was it? More full? More something.

He was looking straight at Thomas. And Thomas was standing like a statue, a cup of half-drunk coffee in his hand, staring. Then Jesus spoke. 'Peace be with you,' he said, straight at Thomas, but the voice swept them all up. Then quietly: 'Thomas, old friend. Here are my hands; touch them. The wound in my side; come and see for yourself. I understand, but there's no need to doubt. Believe me.'

An age passed by and Thomas edged on to the floor.

His hoarse whisper echoed round the silent room. 'My Lord . . . and my God.'

Thomas has always been portrayed as the 50 per cent believer, the man who needed everything proved before he'd believe it. Twenty-first-century man, we've said. We like Thomas, the honest sceptic; he's one of us. Like Woody Allen, who said: 'I don't believe in an afterlife, but I'm bringing a change of underwear.' We live in an age when doubt has become the predominant form of belief.

That's the contemporary dilemma. But is that all there is to Thomas? Or is there something else we need to hear before we load him in with all the world's doubters and agnostics? Let's have a look at another picture of Thomas, only a few days previously. It was when the news had come up-country that Jesus' good friend Lazarus was soon to be no more for this world, and was lying on the edge of death. Jesus was on his way to Bethany, just outside Jerusalem, to be with the family, but there was an understandable nervousness in the camp. The other disciples weren't at all sure that going to Jerusalem was a good idea. Jesus had been making himself pretty unpopular with the House of Bishops and the disciples could see a very sticky end coming their way.

Then it's Thomas who steps out of the shadows. We've hardly heard of him in the rest of the Gospels; just one of a list of disciples. 'The twin', he was called, which doesn't tell us a lot. But now here he is, the man for the moment, and he bursts out with passionate conviction: 'Let's all go, that we may die with him!'

So what is this? Hardly the timid, doubtful figure we've got used to thinking of. Here's a man who's prepared to go to the wire for Jesus. 'Let's go and die with him!' Let's give it all we've got! Let's show what we're made of! Good for you, Thomas. Maybe we've got to reassess our picture of you. Maybe instead of being the 50 per cent believer Thomas is actually the 110 per cent believer, the one who wants to give everything. The one who has so much riding on his commitment to Jesus that he just has to know it's right. He longs to give everything for everything rather than nothing for nothing. He longs to follow Jesus with all his heart and mind and strength. 'Let's go and die with him.' But if Thomas has got all this to give, then he needs to know he's not making a fool of himself. 'Unless I see the mark of the nails . . .'

But when he gets the proof he needs and he sees the risen Lord and feels the overwhelming presence of Christ, there's no stopping him. All his pent-up commitment tumbles out, and his hopes and intuitions are all confirmed. 'Yes! My Lord and my God!' That huge recognition. Thomas was the first person to see that final truth, the divinity of Christ, and to worship him. This is no wimpish faith, no grudging, mealy-mouthed faith; this is red-blooded, high-octane stuff. Would that the Church were full of it! A faith that's less like an abstract discussion and more like a love affair.

That's a big problem today. It's not an age in which people want to make the grand gesture. It's an age which says – hang loose, stay cool, chill out, don't get too committed, keep your options open. And in this kind of culture many Christians too are so laid back they're practically horizontal. They don't want to get too involved. They fear if they come in to help mend a fuse they might end up churchwarden. So if we're going to get stuck into Christianity, there's a lot at stake, and many of us, like Thomas, will want a fair bit of reassurance. It's not that

117

we don't have lots to give. It's just that the culture is against big commitments and heroic failures. So we need to be pretty sure.

I had a friend called Ron. The first time I met him and his wife Sandy his second child had just been killed in a car accident, going to school with his mother. Aged six. Their first child had died of brain damage two years before. Aged four. Not a good basis for someone to feel kindly disposed towards God. But Ron gradually battled his way to faith. A lot was at stake. If he was going to believe, he was going to give it everything, so he had a lot riding on it. He came to what he called a 'fingernail' faith; always hanging on by his fingernails, but that was enough, just enough. And so he did give it everything, and handled our sound system and put on brilliant *son et lumières* and ran a group called No Holds Barred, for other people on the edge of faith. At those groups he and Sandy gave us good company, good discussion and good whiskey. Later they had another son, and what could he be called but – Thomas.

How much is riding on our Christian commitment? How much is at stake? We all know the caricature Christian who seems to take his faith out of a box on Sundays but not to know what to do with it the rest of the week. And we probably know some others who seem to have it all sussed and always to be living in a flurry of devotion and good works. But many of us are probably like Thomas, with lots to give – if we could just be a little more sure, have a little more evidence. Jesus has a special word for us. 'Blessed are those who have not seen and yet have come to believe.'

Dare we take the risk? The promise is that if we take half a step towards Jesus we'll find ourselves putting down the half-drunk cup of coffee, sliding on to the floor and declaring in a hoarse whisper, 'My Lord and my God.' And then the barriers can come down; the last high citadel can be surrendered, and the Christian adventure can begin in earnest.

For personal or group reflection

- Do you dare to admit your doubts, even to yourself?
- Is your doubt a sign of weakness, maturity or lack of information?
- Who would you talk to about your doubts?

Further group activities

- Together identify your main doubts about Christian faith. Then get into threes and let each person air their own concerns and have the others try to answer them. Bring major problems to the whole group at the end, or ask the vicar or minister to come and tackle them next time!
- If doubt is the other side of major commitment, share stories of how members of the group grew in their faith and understanding by facing doubts and problems.

For prayer

- Hold a coin in your hands. With one side of the coin uppermost, pray about the doubts and problems you have in believing. Then turn the coin over and express your longing and love of God and your desire to serve him.

- Pray for anyone you know who has genuine intellectual problems with belief, for the right encounters, the right experiences, and the right books to read.